ISLAM ETHICS AND TEACHINGS

Muhammed Kunju Salim

KITAB BHAVAN
New Delhi-110002

KITAB BHAVAN
Exporters & Importers
1784, Kalan Mahal, Daryaganj
New Delhi-110002 (India)
Phones : 3274686, 3263383
Telex : 31-63106 ALI IN

ISBN 81-7151-111-2

First Edition 1991

Published by
Nusrat Ali Nasri for Kitab Bhavan
1784, Kalan Mahal, Daryaganj
New Delhi-110002 (India)

Printed in India at:
Zubin Offset Printers
2090, Guest House
Rodgaran, Delhi-6

Contents

1. INTRODUCTION

Progress is a never ending entity. With every idea something hitherto unknown to the world is born; the new idea which is absolute truth or nearer to perfection never ceases to exist. Something old falls with every change as the poet sang, "Old order changeth yielding place to new."

Full knowledge about the Creator was beyond human comprehension. The primitive people, unable to solve the mystery of creation had worshipped all those rare phenomena around them–the sun, the moon, the stars, the water, the mountains and even plants and animals. Thus the moon was the lord for sometime, then the sun, stars etc. Azer, the father of Prophet Abraham who is believed to have lived some four thousand years ago had worshipped many gods. As a boy, Abraham too followed him. When night drew its shadow over him, he saw several stars twinkling in the sky. "They are surely my gods", he exclaimed. But when they faded in the morning light, he said, "I will not worship gods that fade." Next he turned to the waning and waxing moon. "This is my Lord." But when it too set, he said, "This too is not my Lord." And when he saw the daily round of the sun, he believed it must be the Great Being. This is bigger than the other two, the stars and the moon. He quickly abandoned it when it too disappeared in the morning sky. (sura VI Cattle) It was this Azer who had initiated making clay images. However, when these mute gods refused to answer their quest for knowledge, his followers turned to explanatory and aesthetic myths and witchcrafts.

Guiding the mankind to the right path, God had sent many messiahs with Divine Messages. Even though they preached Universal Peace and Truth, their teachings vary in essence. There is fundamental difference in the preachings of Hosiah and Amos. Issiah and his contemporary prophet Meccah jointly preached more on foregiveness of God. Six of the several hundred prophets who preached to mankind are dignified with special titles:

Adam (Safiyullah, i.e., The Chosen of God)
Noah (Nabiyullah, i.e., The Preacher of God)
Abraham (Khalilullah, i.e.,The Friend of God)

Mosus (Kalimullah, i.e., The Converser with God)
Jesus (Ruhullah, i.e.,The spirit of God)
Muhammad (Rasulullah, i.e.,The Messenger of God)

One of the later prophets, John Baptist "does not tell the people to give up their job and retire to the forest, he advises them to lead a holy life within their status and profession."[1] Jesus Christ was the prophet of mercy, he was in the fact the Prince of Peace. And still later Prophet, Muhammad who lived in the sixth century, in the full limelight of the history is the Prophet of "the last of the great modern religions to develop" whose teaching is the essence of all previous messages.

We learn that every religion--whether Judaism, Zoroastrianism, Manichaeism, Buddhism or Christianity--is made complete with final prophethood. Jainism is based on the teachings of twenty four Tirthankaras ending with Mahavira Vardhamana who is the last and final leader. He is the real founder of Jainism.Mahayana Buddhists believe not in one Buddha but many, one for each creation of the world. In Zoroastrianism, there is a long line of Zorothustra and the relegion is founded on the last Prophet who is also the greatest. Islam, the youngest of the great religions of the world is perfected with the last and final prophethood of Muhammad (God's Blessings be upon him) and Al-Quran, the Sacred Text of Islam, is "the quintessence of all previous scripts verified and consolidated ."[2] Islam is thus Universal Faith, the Religion of Mankind. "This day have I perfected your religion for you, completed My favour upon you, and have chosen for you Islam as your religion."[3] Thus, God has perfected the religion with the final Prophethood of Muhammad, and Islam is the Chosen Religion of mankind.

A fundamental Islamic teaching is that no Prophet was commanded to establish a religion. Prophets are Warners-pure and simple. God said to Prophet Muhammad: "Your only duty is to give warning. We have sent you with the truth to proclaim good news to warn your people; for there is no nation that has not been warned by an apostle."The prophets carry messages of good conduct and warned the people when they had deviated from truth.

[1]Life of Christ:E. he, Joly S.J.,p.34

[2]Al Quran, Sura Baiyanat 97.23.

[3]Al Quran, Al Maidah 5.4.

The Philosophy of Gautama Buddha who was born in a princely Hindu Kshatriya family was turned into a religious dogma by the moral flabbishness of the people that lived immediately after him. Jesus Christ had never wished to be the founder of a religion named after him. Jesus of Nasreth, the King of the Jews had emphatically said,"Do not think that I have come to set aside the Law and the prophets. I have not come to set them aside. But to bring them to perfection."[4] Dissatisfied with the conflicting ideologies of Hinduism and Islam, Guru Nanak preached moderation, a middle-of- the road policy, but unaware, a new relegion in the name of Sikhism was founded on his teaching. "Zarathustra never calls himself the founder of a religion, but a reformer as did Lao Tse and Kung Tse."[5]

Like Buddha, Jesus Christ, Zarathustra, Lao Tse and Guru Nanak, Muhammad dissatisfied with the primitive outlook and consciouness, social relegious bankruptcy, revolted against then prevailing order and set out for great mission--the mission renovating the society, bringing it back to its former glory, to Truth. Islam was , and is not a new religion. It was the religion of the Adam, Noah , Abraham, Moses and Jesus which in course of time, corrupted itself. Polytheism set in; people become nonbelievers. The messages and warnings of God--sent apostles were disgraded. It was in this world that Prophet Muhammad was born. Unlike other Prophets earlier to him, Muhammad is the seal of the Prophets (Khatimun Nabiyin. Sura 33.40) for he could deliver the Divine message to mankind. "Few events in human history are more remarkable than the sudden appearance and triumph of Islam in the early part of the seventh century of the common era. Within a period of twenty years, what were regarded as the wild tribesman of Arabia conqured a great part of the Eastern Empire of Rome which had been consolidated for nearly a thousand years, dominated Christianity in its orginal home, and established a progressive civil form of government over Arabia, Syria, Mesopotamia, Persia and Egypt. The unification Arabia by the Prophet himself, which preceded this astounding Arab conquest, was scarcely regarded by the rulers of the Roman Empire, but it was miraculous."[6] There appeared that Islam would penetrate deep into Europe. Islam is not confined to Arabia alone. The largest Muslim populations in the world are in non-Arab countries--Indonesia,

[4]Life of Christ by Fulton J. Sheen.
[5]The Living Religions p.391
[6]The Religious Foundations of Internationalism, Morman Bentwic .p.158.

POPULATION

Pakistan, India Bangladesh and the Soviet Union .

Countries	Total	Muslims	Percentage
	Milliions	Millions	
Indonesia	174.0	147.9	85
Pakistan	98.0	95.0	97
India	790.0	94.8	12
Bangladesh	105.0	94.5	90
U.S.S.R.	284.5	51.2	45
Nigeria	89.0	40.0	45
China	1052.0	14.6+	1.4

+on the another account 9% of Chinese are Muslims i.e.93.7 million. Russia is reputed to have 60 million Muslims.

Every one fifth of the world's 5 Billion inhabitants are Muslims. Of all the existing world religions, Islam is the youngest claiming nearly a billion adherents to its faith. "Veriely the true religion in the sight of God is Islam."(Sura III. Imrans) Beginning as a one man movement in the Arabian desert in the middle of the seventh century, it soon gained momentum and within a short span a few decades are crossed the borders. Islam penetrated deep into Europe and from there spread to all the continents. Now hardly a country is left where the Azhan or Call to prayer is not heard. It goes on and off, five times a day from early dawn to dusk and late evening, summoning the Faithfuls for prayer. When the Azhan is heard, Muslims all over the Islamic world stop all the worldy activities to congregate on the quadrangle of any mosque to pray to God with rhythmic uniformity. Whether they hail from the jungles of Africa or the Oasis of the Great Salt Desert or from the distant East or West, they say the same prayers which were taught to them by their leader, the Prophet of Islam in the early part of his Prophetic career. Despite the diversity of the races and languages, food and clothing, Islam unifies all to a Universal Community or Umma. As members of this royal forum, they pray and dine together and assemble from all corners of the world by air, sea and road in Mecca,the First City of Islam, during the sacred month, Dul-Haj for the performance of their life goal, the pilgrimage. Islam prescribes certain duties to its adherents which make tnem disciplined to lead a more responsible life.

The life of the Prophet of Islam has greatly influenced his disciples. They very minutely study all his actions and saying which are guidelines all over the Islamic World. They constantly refer to them when they are in doubt of their own actions and a vast literature of Commentaries of his Sayings and Doings (Hadith) is being established for good conduct.

So much at least of preliminary background is necessary to the understanding of the religion called Islam and its dogmas and teachings.

Now we may pass on to the meaning of Islam. Islam is a verbal noun from "Aslama". The root word is "Salam"which means submission or obedience (to the Will of Allah). It also means peace. Thus we see Islam is (1) Submission to the Will of Allah, and (2) Making Peace. Anyone who trusts Allah and entrusts himself to Him is a Muslim and his religion is Islam. Submission and peace are complementary. Obedience is complete when one submits entirely to God both physically and spiritually, bodily and mentally. Good thoughts and deeds are pre-requisities for peace. Without man maintaining peace himself and with fellow beings, he cannot submit himself to the Eternal Will. Deeds are very important; noble work performed by a person make a man virtous. It is rightly said, Good deed is the best form of prayer." "The smallest service for even a minute is far more valuable than spending the whole of a year in prayers." Virtues, more excellence and goodness deserve reward and those who performed good, noble and excellent works will be rewarded in this world and in the other world as well. So a true Muslim according to the Holy Book is the rightous among men. "It is not rightousness that ye turn your faces towards East or West but it is rightousness to believe in God and in the Last Day and Angles and the book and the Messengers, to spend of your substance out of love for Him, for your kin, for orphans, for the needy for the wayfarer for those who ask and for the ransome of slaves, to be steadfast in prayer and practise regular charity to fulfil the contracts which ye have made and to be firm and patient in pain (or suffering) and adversity and throughout all periods of panic. Such are the people of truth, the God-fearing."[7f] One of the Sayings of the Holy Prophet, defines a Muslim as "one from whose hands, tongue and limbs everyone is safe." In this broad based definition, Muslim inclueds non-Muslims also who are just doers. Who then is not a Muslim?" Verily, he is not a Muslim who fills up his stomach

[7] Al-Quran, Sura Al-Baqara 2. 177.

while his neighbours are starving."[8] This excludes those Muslims who are not Muslims by virtue of their selfishness when their neighbours irrespective of their belief are starving. Quite justifiably, Goethe said, "every thinking man among us is, in fact a Muslim."

Further tracing the genesis of Islam, we can scarcely ignore the Muslim formula of Greeting which also is derived from 'Salam' is the quintessence of Islamic teaching. Upon seeing a person he says,"Assalamu Alaik". In brief, it means `peace be on you' but it has a wider meaning. "Assalam", as seen earlier, derived from 'Salam' meaning 'The Peace', is one of the Attributes of God, In this sense, the Greeting also means 'Allha, the Lord of the peace watching on you'. It is therefore enjoined upon you to maintain peace in the world. Peace is a derivative of mutual love; where there is love, there is also peace, and where there is hatred, there is anger, calamity and war. A Greeting is replied with another, a better greeting. "Wa Alaikum Assalam" (And Peace be on you) or better, "And the Lord of peace is watching on you." Thus Al-Quran says, "If a man greets you, let your greetings be better than his or at least return his greeting."(Sura IV:86)

Saluting is a Fitrah (Incumbent Duty) on every Muslim. Imam Bukhari, the celebrated compiler of Hadith has recorded a Tradition as narrated by Abu Huraira. The Prophet said, "God created Adam in his own likeness, and his stature was 60 cubits, and God said to Adam. 'Go and salute that party of angles who are sitting down, and listen to their answer, for veriley it shall be the salutation and reply for you and your children .'Adam then went and said to the angles, "As-Salamu Alaikum' and the angles replied, 'As-Salamu Alaika wa Rehmuatual-lahi." Returining a greetings is an incumbent duty (Raddu's Salam) on every Muslim and while doing so, both have blessed each other . The sacred script (Sura IV Women) says, "If a man greets you let your greeting be better than his or at least return his greeting."

We now turn to the day to day activities of a Muslim. Usually the pious Muslims begin every good act with a formula, somthing like an ejaction. It is the Basmallah or 'Bismillah'. In full, it is "Bismillahir-Rahmanir-Rahim." (In the name of God, the Compassionate, the Merciful). It is the auspiciatory form in the whole of Islam.

[8]Hadith of Prophet Muhammad.

There is a Prophetic saying that he is reported to have said that the formula Basmallah contains the Surat-al-Fatiha (The chapter of Praise or Opening Sura) which in turn is Quran summed up. Quran itself contains all the previous revelations. How great is Basmallah! How noble and virtuous is the Muslim who pronounces Basmallah many times a day! Quranic Commentators give a wide meaning for this four-word formula. They say it represents the four streams of Paradise. However it contains two of the best attributes of God—Rahman[9] and Rahim[9]. Both have derived from the same root word Rahmah (Mercy), the former depicts God's Intrinsic Mercy and the latter, Extrinsic Mercy. i.e. God the Creator and God the Saviour, two essence of God. Combined with God's other name, Allah[9], Basmallah reflects the three phases of the Divine Infinity.

Bismilla begins with the letter ب (bā) which eventhough the second letter of Arabic Script is the most important for it contains the vital 'Point' (.) corresponding to the first drop of divine ink (Midad) to fall from the pen. Midad is er-Ruh or the Divine Spirit. Without this point below the bowl like curve ب the letter makes no sense. It lost its meaning. This point alone makes the letter what it is. Considering the importance of this point in Bā, Hadhrat Ali Ibn Abu Talib, fourth Caliph said that it symbolises principal unity. In fact ب is second only to ا the first alphabet which stands for Oneness, the vital attribute of Allah.

It is apparent from the above that Bismillah is a very important formula in Islam. In al-Quran, it is used as an Invocation prefixed to all its 114 Suras (Chapter) except the ninth, the popular view for its omission is that it is a chapter of punishment. It is recorded that Prophet Muhammad had never done a thing, however unimportant it might be, without reciting it. All his letters and pledges had begun with this golden formula, and his followers throughout the world scrupulously follow it in all their activities. Every Muslim recites it many times daily. He says it before eating, washing, bathing, wearing new clothes, before undertaking a journey, before marriage and in all his activities. There are many who begin their personal letters with this formula. It is a sign of blessing. In personal letters, it also shows affinity and respect. Instead of writing the whole formula, some write only its numerical values added to 786.

---

[9]None of these can be translated in any other language.

1	ا	1	ا	1	ب
30	ل	30	ل	60	س
200	ر	200	ر	40	م
8	ح	8	ح	1	ا
10	ي	40	م	30	ل
40	م	50	ن	30	ل
				5	ه
289		329		168	

= 289 + 329 + 168 = 786

In the olden days, each Arabic alphabet has a number assigned to it Below is the table of letters vis-a-vis the corresponding number.

Number	Letter	Number	Letter
1	ا	60	س
2	ب	70	ع
3	ج	80	ف
4	د	90	ص
5	ه	100	ق
6	و	200	ر
7	ز	300	ش
8	ح	400	ت
9	ط	500	ث
10	ي	600	خ
20	ك	700	ذ
30	ل	800	ض
40	م	900	ظ
50	ن	1000	غ

2. ETHICS OF ISLAM

The ethical philosophy of Islam is that God is One and He is the supreme Lord of all creation. He has no offspring because He has no consort. He has created the universe and Heavens to reveal Truth. Everything good and evil in this world exists by His Will. A Believer is one who submits to the Divine Will ie. who resigns. The root of the doctrine of Islam is in the beliefs of

(1) *immortality of the soul;*
(2) *the reality of a future life, and*
(3) *predestination.*

The present life is momentary, is a sport and pastime. It is the life to come that is the true life. (Sura 29 Spider). When death approaches a person, on Divine Command, separates his soul from the body. The souls thus separated are preserved until the Last Day, i.e., The Judgement Day when the souls are reunited with the bodies for receiving the eternal reward or punishment which will be decided by the Divine Tribunal. Another Islamic belief is that the blessed souls shall be preserved in a place called *Illiyum* beneath the Throne of God in the seventh heaven and the condemned souls, in the abyss of Hell, *Sidjeen*. Some also believe it is the same prison where the Register of the actions and thoughts of the wicked is kept until the Day of resurrection. On the basis of the earthly deeds, a person shall be judged before the Great Tribunal. The Righteous shall dwell in an eternal bliss for ever and the wicked shall become heirs to the hell-fire where they are burnt for their misdeeds. They shall not expect any respite from the punishment. "Whoever has done an atom's weight of good shall see it, and whoever has done an atom's weight of evil shall see it also." (Sura 99. The Earthquake). Islam believes in absolute predestination, i.e., everything happens as decreed and pre-determined by God which is written in the Perspicuous Book. It is a Preserved Table wherein God's decrees are recorded. It contains everything from "the minutest to the biggest happened and going to happen." (Sura 6 Cattle). No soul dies without the permission of God, according to what is written in the Book containing the determination of things, i.e., every man's birth, action, thoughts, deeds and death are decreed and pre-determined by God (Sura

III Imrans). "God knoweth that which is on the dry land and in the sea; there falleth no leaf, but He knoweth it; neither is there a simple grain in the dark parts of the earth, neither a green thing, nor a dry thing, but it is written in the Perspicuous Book." (Sura VI. Cattle).

God, through His several revelations right from Adam through Noah, Abraham, Issa to the last of His Messenger, Muhammad, on them be Peace, has clearly distinguished truth from vices, good from evils. A rightly guided man is a believer who leads a good life within the precincts of Islamic Law which earns him a better life after death. Essentially Islamic Law is Divine Law. The Umma of Believers or the Muslim Society is formed of all those Faithfuls who are rightly governed by a Code of Life called the Shariah which is a complete set of rules and regulations for all times. It sanctions, recommends and prescribes what is just; it regulates, condemns, disfavours and prohibits what is unjust.

We have already seen that the root of Islamic concept of Life is based on the fact that everything belongs to God. He is the only Creator. He is all Powerful; He is Omnipresent and Omniscient. He sees all and hears all and knows everything. He has no consort, and free from all mistakes, weaknesses and faults. God alone knows about the past, present and future. He only knows the Five Keys of Secret Knowledge—The Time of the Day of Judgment; The Time of Rain; What is forming in the wombs—male or female; What shall happen in the Future, and Where any person shall die. (Sura XXXI Lokman). Man, as one of the creation has to live in complete obedience to Him. Such a man is a Believer or Mo'min who has been shown the right path of virtues (Ma'rufat) and who has been guided to refrain from vices (Munkarat). In other words, a Muslim's approach to God is straight and direct. God watches him all times. He knows the furtive looks and all thoughts concealed in his mind and so no man can escape from Him. Man is always under the alert eyes of His Lord. He is nearer to man than his own jugular vein (Sura L). "There are guardians watching over you, noble recorders who know of all your actions." (Sura 82. The Cataclysm). Again, "for every soul there is a guardian watching over it." (Sura 86 The Nightly Visitant). This fearness and alertness in him that he is watched by his Lord cultivates in him an inner urge to do good because he is answerable for all his actions. Only his deeds alone save him from the Divine Wrath.

Every human being will be put to trial on the basis of his belief, actions and utterances. So Islam enjoins upon its votaries to make the present life as glorious as possible for which a detailed moral conduct is prescribed in the Shariah which derive its precepts from the Sacred Text and Sunnah of the Holy Prophet. In fact one of the chief reasons for the success of Islam in so short a period was the ethics and moral precepts contained in Al-Quran and Sunnah which together form the Doctrinal Source of Islam which governs all phases of human life from small details of personal and domestic life to broad aspects of his civic conduct and national and international behaviour. Also Muslims are governed by several Adab books which prescribe moral instruction on silence, humility, tranquility and steadfastness besides admonishing them from vices like envy, greed, frivolity and prodigality.

In order to maintain the continuity of narration, I must describe briefly what part the Sacred Text and Sunna has on the everyday life of a Muslim.

Al-Quran

The Quran is the Sacred Text of the Muslims who believe that a copy of it existed together with the whole life of the world in a table called Al Lawh Al-Mahfuz in Paradise from all eternity. From there, it descended to the lower heaven and was conveyed to the Prophet part by part in varying length through the Archangel Gabriel in a period of his twenty two years of Prophetic career. It is possible that most of the verses of al-Quran were recorded during the life time of the Prophet and it is also possible that most of his companions had learnt them by heart. It is known now that about 102 educated companions of the Prophet were knowing by heart verses if not fully partially as revealed to the Prophet. Most of them were knowing only few verses, but it is obvious that few of them could recite every syllable of the Quran. But in the subsequent campaigns especially in the military expedition of Bir Mauna during the life time of the Prophet, and Yamama during the Caliphate of Abu Bakr most of the Quran reciters were slain. This arose the attention of Abu Bakr who had appointed Zayd ibn Thabit, the chief amanuensis of the Prophet to compile and codify the Quran. The Sacred Text so compiled was the official copy of Quran and was kept with Abu Bakr on whose death it passed on to Umar, the second Caliph. When he died, it went into the hands of Hafsa, the Prophet's widow. During the Caliphate of Hadhrat Uthman different forms of recitations were reported from Emessa, Damascus in Syria, Kufa and

Basra in Iraq. Several copies of the Quran, copied from the official copy which was in the custody of Hafsa, were made by a committee under the leadership of Zayd ibn Thabit assisted by Abd Allah ibn Al Zubir, Sa'id ibn al As and Abd Al Rahman ibn Al Harith. Certified copies of these Quran were sent to all provinces of Islam followed by an official order to destroy the unauthorised copies. Quran ever since that day kept its pristine purity.

Islamic belief is that every nation has a warner to deliver the Divine Message. "We have sent no apostle but with the language of his people" (Quran 14.4). God has sent down 104 scriptures—50 revealed to Seth (Shith), 30 to Idris, 20 to Abraham, 1 to Moses, 1 to David, 1 to Issa, and 1 to Mohammed—and the knowledge contained in all the sarced books was distributed among the Torah, Gospel, Psalms and Quran. In fact, Quran excels all, and contains the wisdom of the remaining three. And God has deposited the knowledge of Al Quran in the Fatiha (Sura 1) and anyone who knows the meaning of Fatiha knows the exigesis of Quran who in turn knows the exigesis of Torah, Gospel and Psalms, and all other scriptures. Quran surpasses all others in enumerating the past events and in giving a graphic account of the future. It contains Unity, Praise and Glorification of Lord, beliefs in his apostles and prophets. It incites good works, and prohibits evils, exhorts heaven.

Quran is undoubtedly one of the world's classics, read and re-read by Muslims all over the world. Five times a day, they recite its opening Sura in every Ra'ka of the prayer besides saying a few other verses. Millions all over the world read it every day, many learn it. Year after year, many editions of Al-Quran appear and all of them find buyers as quickly as they are printed. Some of them are so small that two or more of them can be neatly packed in a match box. Some others have printed all its 6200 verses in a sheet of paper.[1]

Quran means recitation is the "word of Allah" as transmitted to the Prophet through the Archangel Gabriel.

> *Recite In the Name of thy Lord who created Man of a blood-clot.*
>
> *Recite: And thy Lord is the Most Generous, who taught by the Pen taught Man that he knew not" (Quran 96.1-5).*

---

1. or 77,638 words, i.e., 323,015 letters set in 114 Suras

Al-Quran teaches men to glorify God whose power and benefices are abound everywhere. God is One and only One. This message of Unity of God is revealed to many passages in the Text.

> *"Say, God is one God; the enternal God: he begetteth not, neither is he begotten and there is not anyone like unto him" (Quran CXII : 1-5).*

This is again repeated in the *"Throne Verse"*[2]

> *"God! there is no God but He; the living the self-subsisting*
> *Neither slumber nor sleep seizeth him;*
> *To Him belongeth whatsoever is in heaven, and on earth*
> *Who is He that can intercede with Him, but through His good pleasure.*
> *He knoweth that which is past, and that which is to come unto them,*
> *And they shall not comprehend anything of His knowledge, but so far as he pleaseth.*
> *His throne is extended over heaven and earth, and the preservation of both is no burden unto Him.*
> *He is the high, the mighty. (Quran II.256)*

As we shall see, of the other moral principles, Prohibition of wine occupies a prominent place (Sura II. 219 & V. 90). Wine is an abomination to God and Islam has succeeded where legislation has failed in banishing one of the greatest evils of mankind. Few Muslims drink liquor. Prohibition is such a complete denial in Islam that even possessing money obtained from liquor sale is a great sin. Pressing grapes for making wine is also unlawtul. Prohibited things include opium, bhang, tobacco and certainly coffee as the fumes of coffee cause one to lose his thinking and reasoning power. Casting of lots, and chance opening of Al-Quran and similar other sacred texts and magic too are condemned. (Some commentators believe that as chess playing requires skill, it is permitted to Muslims.)

We also find in the Quran certain virtues exhorted, certain vices condemned and certain regulations merely recommended. All the suras of Al-Quran especially Suras 2,4 and 5 have many passages of exhor-

---

[2] These seven verses are so important that some pious Muslims engrave them on agates or stones and amulets and wear it about them to ward of evil.

tations, namely "Deal not unjustly with others, and ye shall not be dealt with unjustly." *(Sura II)*

"Covet not that which God hath bestowed on some of you preferably to others."

"Show kindness unto parents, relations, orphans, and the poor, and also to your neighbour, to your friend, the traveller, and the captives when your right hand shall possess."

"O true believers! Observe justice when ye appear as witness before God, and let not hatred towards any individual induce to do wrong."

"Verily the most honourable of you, in the sight of God, is the most pious of you." (Sura XLIX)

Other virtues exhorted are Humility (Sura XVII - 239, XXV-6, XXVIII-83 and XXXI - 18)

Honesty (Sura XVII - 37, LV - 8 & LXXXIII 2 - 3)

Alms giving (Sura XXIV - 22, XXIV 61 LXXIV - 6, II, III, IV, VI, VII, IX, XIV, XIX, XIII, XXVIII, XXXI, XXXII) etc.

Kindness (Sura IV - 40, VI - 152 & XVII 24 - 25, XLVI)

Trustworthiness (Sura IV - 62, V - 1, VIII 27 - 28, XXIII 2 & 9 & XXV 72 & 73)

Friendship (Sura XVII), Piety (Sura XLIX), Obedience to Parents (Sura XLVI, XXXI, XXIX, XLII, L, LVIII, LVII etc.)

Other recommended virtues are visiting the sick, generosity, participation in social work, bravery, honesty, loyalty, cleanliness, love of neighbours, respect to elders and kindness to youngsters, patience etc.

Vices that are condemned are Boasting (Sura XXXI: 2-17)

"And do not turn your face away from the people in contempt, not go about in the land exulting over much; surely Allah does not love self conceited boaster."

On Pride Al-Quran says *"Surely Allah does not love him who is proud, boastful."* (Sura IV: 36)

"And do not go about in the land exultingly." (Sura XVII: 37) Blashpemy (Sura XXXIII: 57) Slander (Sura XXXIII 38, CIV) Infanticide (Sura XVII: 33), Adultery (Sura XVII: 34, XXIV), Cheating in Trade (Sura XVII: 37), Usury (Sura XXX), Hoarding (Sura CIV, XXVIII), Defraud (Sura III), Fornication (Surs IV).

Al-Quran says of a Judgment Day when all the dead will arise to receive eternal fate. "And because the Hour will come, there is no doubt there of, and because Allah will raise those who are in the graves." (Sura XXV). The wicked will go to Hell, the Blessed, to heaven. The Sacred Text is severe to thieves, robbers, slanderers and adulterers. "As for the thief, both male and female, cut off their hands. It is the reward of their punishment from Allah." (Sura V-38). To inflict this punishment, Sunna prescribes the theft value to be four dinars and the recommended punishment for repeating the offence is on stages—to amputate the right hand at the wrist for the first offence and left foot at the ankle for the second offence. If the cirminal repeats a third time, he will lose his left hand and the fourth time, his right foot. If he does not stop and continues the crime, flogging is suggested. It is preferable to punish a thief, an adulterer or a drunkard publicly in the presence of not less than three persons. Theft is serious an offence in Islam, there is a Prophetic Saying, "If Fatema, the daughter of Muhammad steal, let her hand be struck off." (More Quranic verses on Sura V and XXIV). There is a tradition which narrates that Prophet had said, "whoever cheateth another will on the Day of Judgement carry his fraudulent purchase publicly on his neck."

It also prescribes severe punishment for those who are guilty of lewdness (Sura IV-15). They should be scourged with hundred strips. (Sura XXII - 2). Similarly, those who bring false accusation against honourable women are punishable with eighty strips. (Sura XXIV-4). Intoxicants including opium and tobacco and unclean food such as pork, carrion, blood and those animals or birds which die a natural death or killed by any other animal (Sura II, Sura V) are forbidden to eat of lust but permissible on extreme necessity to save one's life from hunger etc. However wool and hair of such animals are pure, only skin and bones are impure. Lawful meat is that which is slaughtered by cutting the windpipe and gullet through, repeating at the same time, "In the name of Allah, Allah is great". The following are considered to be not impure.

1. Animals like fish which constantly live in water. There is a prophetic saying that "sea water is pure, and the bodies which live in water are premissible food."
2. Animals which do not have blood (provided) they are not generated in filth.
3. Man.

The Recommended Regulations occur in almost all suras. They cover all aspects of human behaviour. The Sacred Text teaches the Faithful, how to enter a house and depart from a house (Sura XXIV 28-29). "Believers, do not enter the dwellings of other men until you have asked their owners' premission and wished them peace. That will be best for you."

"If you find no one in them, do not go in till you are given leave. If you are refused admission, it is but right that you should go away."

Clear instruction is given on Privacy (Sura XXIV 57). Quran gives three occasions when even domestic servants and children obtain permission to come to one's presence because these are the probable times one needs privacy.

"Believers, let your slaves and children ask your leave when they come in to see you before the morning prayer, when you have put off your garments in the heat of noon, and after the evening prayer. These are the three occasions when none may intrude upon you."

Protection to Orphans (Sura II 219, IV4 - 7, XVII 36) is encouraged to almost a religious duty. Similarly one can read clear injunction on Nursing and Weaning (Sura II 233). Reconciliation (Sura IV 128 - 129, IV 8 & 9) on Marriage (Sura IV), Inheritance (Sura IV 8 & 11, 14) Brotherhood (Sura XXXIII. 5 - 6) Almsgiving (Sura XXIV 22, XXIV 16 etc.) and Enemies (Sura LXIV 14).

God is severe in punishing; swift is God in punishment. Many were the races who were destroyed for their obstinacy, wickedness and unbelief. The Sacred Script gives the history of many such tribes. Adites, the people of gigantic strength and stature were unconcerned to the Divine Warning of Hud, their Prophet. God drove a cloud of destruction over their land followed by a violent wind which destroyed the whole people save only the righteous. The Thamudites, another race were overpowered by a terrible earthquake with a loud explosion and thunder. Before dawn, they lay dead in their own mansions which they cut out in the rocks. The people of Babel, the urban people of the twin cities of Sodome and Gomorroh, the inhabitants of Midain all perished because of their hardened unbelief.

The orthodox view is that "Al-Quran is divine, uncreated, from Him it issued and to Him it shall return".[3] Along with the vast com-

---

[3] This was debated and re-debated, and still a bone of contention in Islam. Those

mentaries, it governs the conduct of Believers. It is everything to the Muslims. It regulates the way of life in this world as well as the life hereafter. It covers Tauhid or Declaration of the Unity of God, Ahbar (or histories of earlier Prophets etc.), Diyanat (Regulations), Tadkir (Exhortation), and Ahkam (Law). The former two i.e. Tauhid and Ahbar form the theological principles of Islam and the others, moral principles.

Because of the importance of Quran in the lives of Muslim Community a vast literature was formed on Quran Exegesis (Tafsir), Quranic Criticism (Qiraat) and Scholastic Theology (Kalam). Its theology, its moral principles and jurisprudence supplemented and elaborated by Sunna form the basis of Ethics of Islam and is the primary root of the Faith of Islam.

THEOLOGICAL PRINCIPLES

Al Quran contains in beliefs in One God, in Angels, in Eternal Decrees, in Prophets and Scriptures, in the Intermediate of souls, in the Resurrection, in the Eternal Punishment and in Paradise. It is contained in Sura 4:135. "O true Believers, believe in God and His apostle and the Book which He hath formerly sent down. And whosoever believeth not in God, and His Angels, and His Scriptures, and His Apostles, and the Last Day, he surely erreth in a wide mistake." These beliefs are the root of the Faith of Islam. Al-Quran teaches the monotheistic dogma in its purest form. The Meccan suras which are the early revelations emphasize the Unity of God (Tauheed) while the Medinan Suras (the later revelations) mostly prescribe maxims of practical life. Man as the created must know his Creator (Sura XVII 23) and has a duty to Him. Not associating anything with Allah, nor equalising Him with anything else, is the first and foremost duty of human beings. God, that is Allah had created man with moral responsibility to know the Truth and that there is a Day of Judgement when his actions are valued to reward the just and punish the unjust. Quran also teaches to believe in angels and jinn, in the prophets, important of them being Adam, Noah, Abraham, Lot, Ismael, Moses, Isah and Muhammad, and revealed Books, Taurat, Injil and Al-Quran, and Predetermination.

---

who held the view that 'Al-Quran is created' were condemned as heretics. However, Ahmed ibn Hanbal (d. 241/855) asserts that "the speech of God is of God and is not separate from Him."

MORAL PRINCIPLES

Quran also contains a high tone of morals which teach the Muslims of their social duties. They are either specific regulations for moral conduct or Exhortation to virtue. The former consists of Prayer (Salah).

Fasting (Saum)
Alms giving (Zakat)
Pilgrimage (Hajj)

Together with Confession of Faith (Shahadah) which is the theology of Al-Quran, these four specific regulations form the Five Pillars of Islam or the theoretical duties prescribed to Muslims. (details have been given in Chapter IV).

We are already aware that Islam is a religion of peace. All its dogmas and teachings emanate from peace and Muslims are advised to practise the principles of toleration to fellow beings. Muslims had shown this restraint, this toleration and love to fellow beings from the pinnacle of glory and in many places they were received as the real saviours. Islam enjoins upon its followers to observe utmost restraint in warfare. It has prescribed certain formulas how to wage war, how to treat the prisoners, how to distribute booty etc. It is stern against killing peaceful population, wanton destruction of dwellings and houses, slaying the old and children. Felling trees, destroying gardens and cultivation are discouraged. At the same time, Islam reminds its votaries "to fight those who fight against you but transgress not by attacking them first, for God loveth not the transgressors." (Sura II 190-91). This is one of the outstanding contribution of Islam to modern warfare. While disapproving offensive wars, it sanctions it on self defence only. This permission to fight the enemies ruthlessly, to fight the trangressors tooth for tooth, eye for eye is almost considered as an essential religious duty in the name of God and truth and for the establishment of peace among the mankind. This is Jehad which means one's power to repel the enemy. In its wider sense, it includes every act for the propogation of truth i.e. Islam. Jehad is a recognised form of preaching, preaching with tongue as well as with force. In this broad sense, Jehad recognises all activities with tongue, pen and sword for the propogation of one's faith and belief. The highest form of Jehad is one's supreme sacrifice of his own life for the establishment of truth, for the sake of his own belief. In this special sense, Jehad allows a Muslim as a unit to fight for their religion if they are attacked or are under threat. However, this permission is on defence only and compulsory to the community as a whole. In other words if they fail in this incumbent duty the entire community is blamed. This is Fard Al-Kifaya i.e. individuals are exempted if others participate in it. If all fail, it is a total failure in one of their essential duties and all are jointly responsible for the failure. On such occasion, it is binding on the Faithfuls entirely to fight the aggressors.

ISLAMIC JURISPRUDENCE

In Islam, ethics and jurisprudence, morality and law are so fused together that it is impossible to write about one without referring to the other. Islamic Jurisprudence, while forbiding all rites which are alien to Islamic teaching, had retained many useful ancient customs and practices suitably modified, so far as ones duties to himself, to his family and to fellow beings (Mu'malat) are concerned. At the same time, Islam is an uncompromising religion for the observance of religious precepts (Ibadat).

Now let us see, how these regulations guide the Muslim Community. They are expressed in five legal categories or Ahkam, Fard (Wajib), Mandub, Mubah, Makruh and Haram.

1. Fard (Wajib). Those duties compulsory to every Muslim and whose performance is meritorious and earns him reward are Fard or Wajib. Conversely its omission is punishable. They are two, Fard Ayn and Fard Kifaya. The duties such as ritual worship, fasting, almsgiving etc. which bind individually to each and every Muslim is Fard Ayn while the latter is applicable to the Community as a whole. Its omission is permitted only when others do it. If all failed, the entire community is blameworthy and punishable. Jehad is Fard Kifaya.

2. *Mandub or Mustahab.* Covers the recommended duties, if performed will be rewarded. But however, its omission has no punishment. Recommended worship, any fasting other than Fard Saum, Umra or Lesser Pilgrimage etc. form this cetegory of duties.

3. Permitted or Sanctioned Duties (Mubah). Whose actions have no reward nor punishment are Mubah (Ja'iz).

4. Makruh are duties disliked and disapproved by law. They approach to unlawful and so recommended not to do it. There is however no penalty if performed.

5. As *Haram* are forbidden acts, Muslims are strictly warned of them. It is a great sin to do them, if performed will bring punishment.

Sins are two, Great or Mortal Sins (Kabirah) and Minor Sins (Saghirah). Minor Sins are inherent in human beings in their behaviour and character and are punishable less severely. But Great Sins are unpardonable and deserve severe punishments. But in neither case, the penalty does not wipe away the offence, for the sinners, whether minor or severe, will receive punishment in the next world as well. The orthodox believe that doers of severe misdeeds, will be punished in purgatorial hell.

Great Sins are Seventeen:

1. Infidelity;
2. Despairing of God's mercy;
3. Considering oneself safe from His wrath;
4. Bearing false witnesses;
5. Constantly committing minor sins;
6. False charging a Muslim with adultery;
7. Taking a false oath;
8. Drinking wine;
9. Practising magic;
10. Defrauding orphans of their property;
11. Usury;
12. Committing adultery;
13. Unnatural crimes;
14. Stealing;
15. Murder;
16. Cowardice in battle with infidels;
17. Disobedience to parents,

Al-Beidawi, based on a tradition of Prophet reckons only seven grievous sins:

1. Idolatry
2. Murder
3. False accusing of modest women
4. Adultery
5. Wasting the substance of orphans
6. Taking usury
7. Disobedience to parents. But Ibn Abbas says that mortal sins number about seven hundred. Greatest of them all is 'idolatry' which God will not pardon. (Sura IV). Quran says, "if ye turn aside from the

grievous sins, we will cleanse you from your smaller faults". (Sura IV Women).

Having considered in brief the various regulations that form the basis of Islamic Jurisprudence, let us trace the rules regarding family and social law (Maulat) and Penal Law (Uqubat).

FAMILY AND SOCIAL LAW

Marriage

Islamic social order begins from a family and several such families constitute the Islamic Society. A family is formed when a man and a woman agree to live as husband and wife. Islamic Divine Law or Shariah prescribes elaborate rules and regulations how such a family to be constituted. The only Islamic recognised form of this relationship is Marriage.

There is a Prophetic Saying: Marriage is half the faith. Quran strictly forbids monasticism; celibacy is condemned. In Islam, marriage is a contract agreed upon by two parties, husband and wife. It is a civil contract based on their mutual consent witnessed by two legal witnesses. The husband, if reached puberty gives his consent himself and on behalf of the girl, her father or grand father or brother of the father or any other close relation obtains her consent and pass it on to the husband. There is also a dowry called Mehr as agreed upon prior to the marriage to be given by the husband. The wife gets two-thirds of it at the time of contract. Islamic law recognises her independent status and even after marriage, she can own and inherit property, sell or mortgage her property independent of her husband or children. The marriage is usually celebrated with a simple ceremony, recitation of Fatiha followed by a sermon. Then in the presence of two witnesses the terms are pronounced.

The Religious Text has also clear injunction on the other aspects of marriage. It limits the number of wives one used to have in pre-Islamic days. If law is for all people and for all times, polygamy and not rigid monogamy is the law. Islam has suitably modified the polygamous marriages then prevalent in Arabia with strict religious restraints. Of course, monogamy is universal but it is not necessary always that both the marital partners would be happy. As an outlet for the marriages which end in frustration because of infidelity, insanity, incurable diseases etc. Islam has allowed polygamous marriages restraining the number of wives to four provided one can be impartial to all his wives and has the means to protect them well. If one takes a second wife, he should care them well. Indeed, very few can go for this luxury with so much religious restraints. In Islam also monogamy is the rule and polygamy an exception. On this subject, one thing ought to be said that as a result of religious sanction for limited polygamy, adultery is less frequent in Islam.

But now its meanings are lost to many of our brethren. They scrupulously follow the Quranic Injunction regarding the number of wives one could have, throwing to winds the qualifying part of equal treatment to all his wives. In the name of Quranic sanction of limited polygamy, marriage has become a good pastime for them. By reckless additions in the harem, they ruin their own families. It is against these people, Islam fought a relentless war and, like it or not, the evil is survived as a great threat to the very concept of Islam. Generalising Islam on their misdeeds is totally unjustifiable. In all religions 'these some' are the perverted, and pose many problems to the society. Other Muslims are good husbands to their wives and lead a fully contended monogamous marriage. They are the real Muslims. It is about them and their marriages that the Prophet said, "Marriage is half the faith."

There is also strict Quranic injunction regarding marriages between blood relations. Thus forbidden are the marriages with one's mother, father's wives, one's own daughters, sisters, paternal and maternal aunts, brother's and sister's daughter, foster-mothers, foster-sisters, mother-in-laws, step daughters (under one's own charge) and son's wives. Also prohibited to marry two or more sisters at the same time. By prescribing elaborate rules of marriage, Islam strictly forbids all extra matrimonial relations. Guarding the Muslims from not slipping into the abyss of vices and immorality, Islam discourages free mixing of men and women, obsenities etc. In order to strengthen a good society, Islam strongly disapproves celibacy and asceticism.

Since Islam allows ample legal outlets in the institution of marriage to the extent of tolerating limited polygamy, and extra marital relationship is severely condemned. It prescribes severe punishment to adultery. "The adulterer and the adulterness shall each be given a hundred lashes." (Sura XXIV 2). If they are married people, the recommended punishment according to Sunna is stoning. Earlier a more stringent punishment was suggested i.e. to jail them separately until death (Sura IV). This was later abrogated to stoning. However Islam views adultery, sodomy, fornication and all other similar vices seriously and stringent punishments are given. "Let not compassion towards them prevent you from executing the judgement of God....and let some of the true believers be witnesses of their punishment." (Sura XXIV). In accordance with this Quranic injunction, all punishments are meted out in public in the presence of at least three persons.

As seen earlier, Islam accepts family as the basic unit which constitute husband, wife and children, each has rights and duties of their own. From cradle to grave, each one's rights are clearly defined. Islam never accepts any discrimation or preference. "Your wives are a garment unto you, and ye are a garment unto you." (Sura II Cow). Its people are governed by a uniform law and subjected to Judgement by an impartial Divine Tribunal on the basis of the wordly deeds.

"Verily the Muslims of either sex, and the true Believers of either sex, and the devout men, and the devout women, and the men of veracity, and the women of veracity, and the patient men, and the patient women, and the humble men, and the humble women, and the almsgivers of either sex, and the men who fast, and the women who fast, and the chaste men, and the chaste women, and those of either sex who remember God frequently, for them both God prepared forgiveness and a great reward."(Sura XXXIII. The Confederate)

All children must be equal to a father. Giving preferences among children is strictly prohibited. During pre-Islamic days, females were buried alive, allowing only boys to grow. This, according to the Divine Law is an unpardonable crime, a vice which no civilised society dare to do it. Islam admonishes these cruel fathers, "You shall not kill your children for fear of want. We will provide for them and for you. To kill them is a great sin.'' (The Night Journey. Sura XVII; Women Sura IV).

Quran has many references about the duties of children to their parents. "We have enjoined man to show kindness to his parents. "(Al Ahquaf Sura 46, Luqman. Sura 31, Spider Sura 29). Again it says, "Verily the most honourable of you in the sight of God is the most pious of you."

Divorce

In the pre-Islamic Arabia, marriage and divorce were so frequent and common that men had dozens of marriages and had an equal number of divorces. Husband could repudiate all his wives any time when he was bored of their company. On no circumstances women could divorce the husband. With the advent of Islam, this practice came to an end. As in inheritance, Al-Quran had recognised woman's right in divorce. At the same time, it had restricted the number of wives a man could have to four.

It is to be known that Islam permits divorce on valid reasons. At the same time Muslims were warned of its evil. A prophetic saying is that of all the permitted things, Divorce is the most undesirable. "With Allah, the most detestable of all the things permitted is divorce." In order to discourage it, the Sacred Text prescribes the following restraints. Firstly, a husband can not divorce his pregnant wife. To repudiate a pregnant wife, he has to wait until delivery. Secondly, the wife is entitled for a stipulated sum called Mehr (Dower) if he divorces her. Thirdly, the intention to divorce must be pronounced when the wife is in a state of purity and cleanliness. That is, when she is clean after her menstrual period and the husband had no sexual intercourse with her. Fourthly, the divorce should be given in the presence of two male witnesses. Fifthly, the woman should pass a waiting period (Iddat) of three menstrual periods in her husband's house maintained by him. (Sura Baqarah 228). With the third menstrual period passing over, woman is unlawful to him. But during the period of Iddat, the husband can accept her back as wife. Even after the Iddat period is over, there is nothing in the religious law which debars him to remarry her with her consent. This is the first revocable divorce.

We suppose, both the spouces patched up their differences and agreed to live together. If the marriage per chance slips into rough sea and the spouces find it not smooth, and miserable, Sharia permits another revocable divorce in the manner described earlier. This is the second revocable divorce. The husband can revoke his earlier decision during when she is observing Iddat. Or if the Iddat period is over, he can remarry her after obtaining her willingness.

If the marriage fails again on a third time, the husband can divorce her for a third time but he loses the right of revocation nor can he remarry her even after the Iddat period unless the woman is remarried by another husband and has been divorced by him or in the event he dies. (Sura Baqarah 230).

Elaborate prescriptions are given in the Quran, Sura II and Sura IV for divorce which disfavours any rash and hasty renunciation of one's wife. All efforts should be made for reconcilliation between the two of their own or through their representatives and mediators. To save the ship of marriage from a possible wreck, even mild flogging is permitted.

The waiting period for a wife whose marriage is consummated is three menstrual periods to ascertain whether she carries a baby in her former husband or not. Husband also gets more time to reconcile his decision to divorce his wife. For a wife who is pregnant, the Iddat is until her delivery. Waiting period for a woman whose husband is deceased is four months and ten days as she is wearing mourning cloak. If the woman is not menstruating the period of Iddat is three lunar months from the day the divorce is given.

Many Muslims know only Divorce of Bid'ah or Innovative Divorce which is unislamic. By this, three divorces are pronounced at one time at a stretch and the husband finds satisfaction in divorcing his wife permanently closing the door of reconciliation.

Orphans

We have already seen that kindness and love are pre-requisites for peace. Quran says: "Show kindness to your parents, and relatives, and orphans and the poor, and to your neighbour who is of kin to you and also to your neighbour who is stranger and to your fellow companions, and the traveller and to the slaves who are under your charge, for God never love the proud and vainglorious who are covetous and enjoins others convetousness also. "(Sura IV). Quran restricts and even forbids men to be harsh with children especially with orphans. (Sura II & IV)

> "Again give the orphans when they came of age their substances: and render them not in exchange bad for good: and devour not their substance by adding it to your substance; for this is a great sin." (Sura IV) "To deal righteously with them (Orphans) is best; and if ye intermeddle with the management of what belongs to them, do them no wrong; they are your brethren." (Sura II)

Inheritance

In the Quran certain versus of Sura IV (Women) deal with the Inheritance which form the basis of Islamic Law of Inheritance. "Men shall have a share in what their parents and kinsmen have, whether it be little or much, they are legally entitled to their share. If relatives, orphans or needy men are present at the division of an inheritance, give

---

[3]Religious scholars are not unanimous in this. Some say it amounts to 3 divorces. Others say it is one divorce and is revocable. I personally believe that it counts as one divorce only and is revocable.

them too a share of it, and speak to them kind words. "This abolished once for all a pre-Islamic custom of disallowing women and children in inheriting the father's or husband's wealth on the pretext that they could not participate in the defence of the tribe. In the pagan world, inhertiance was allowed to the participants of war only. God has commanded thus, "A male shall inherit twice as a female. If there be more than two girls, they shall have two-thirds of the inheritance; but if there be one only, she shall inherit the half. Parents shall inherit a sixth each, if the deceased has a child; but if he leaves no children and his parents be his heirs, his mother shall have a third. If he has two brothers, his mother shall have a sixth after payment of his debts and any legacies he may have bequeathed."

"You shall inherit the half of your wives' estate if they die childless. If they leave children, a quarter of their estate shall be yours after payment of their debts and any legacies they may have bequeathed."

"Your wives shall inherit one quarter of your estate if you die childless. If you leave children, they shall inherit one-eighth after payment of your debts and any legacies you may have bequeathed."

"If a man or a woman leave neither children nor parents and have a brother or a sister, they shall each inherit one-sixth. If there be more, they shall equally share the third of the estate, after payment of debts and any legacies that may have been bequeathed, without prejudice to the rights of the heirs." (Sura IV-Women)

Other Moral Restraints

Will and promise to pay a debt must be made in the presence of two witnesses (Sura V 106). Perjury is a crime and is punishable (Sura XXIV 4). Murder is condemned and is a Grave Sin. Retaliation, though sanctioned is discouraged.

The very essence of Islamic Jurisprudence is that penalty never obliterates offence because the sinner and wrongdoer will receive punishment in the next world as well. For theft, amputation of limb is suggested. (Sura V: 38). Armed robbery, the greatest evil in ancient Arabia, or brigandage is punishable with death. The penalty for adultery is one hundred strokes for both man and woman. Death penalty is prescribed for Apostacy (Ridda). Usury is forbidden. Wine is taboo (Sura II: 219 & V: 90). For drinking wine, the offender is punishable with eighty strokes with whip. Dead and strangled animals, blood, swine, animals felled or killed by accident or killed unceremoniously without saying the name of God or killed by other animals are prohibited.

Islamic rules, regulations and prescriptions are a sure remedy to one's weaknesses or to supplement one's deficiency. They make the votaries to grow with the law and lead a perfect and glorious life within the framework of religion. In brief, Islamic Law of marriage and divorce, its prescription of food and prohibition of wine, gambling, usury, casting lots etc. and its recommendation of respecting elders, kindness to parents, to the kith and kin, to all the neighbours, its admonition to be pious and jealous and its contempt of robbery, theft, adultery etc. provide enough outlets so that a person's passion and necessity can be well accommodated within the framework of law. That is the greatest achievement of Islam.

Sunna

Next to the Sacred Text and its commentaries, the vast literature of Sunna regulates a Muslim of his conduct towards the fellow beings. Literally, Sunna is custom; but as a source of Islam, it is the custom of the Prophet and his companions which is compiled from the narrators and referred as models to determine the ceremonial duties, legal practices and beliefs, and all other affairs of human life. Thus, the Sayings and Doings of the Apostle of Allah and his personal habits and that of his companions that were embodied in Sunna is studied and imitated for good and perfect conduct by the Muslims all over the world. Sunna as a matter of fact completes and explains the Quran. During the lifetime of the Prophet, he was the religious and the temporal head. He was the Imam, leading his followers in prayer and the Judge and the Commander. His verdict was law. After his death for some time his followers did not feel the depth of his absence, for they strictly followed the decisions of their master. Luckily, the problems in the ancient society were limited and they had decided cases based on the Sayings and Doings of the Prophet. As years rolled on, they faced many new problems for which the oral narrations of the Traditions found little answer. To mitigate this situation, many pseudo-Traditions became popular. However, oral narration at last gave way to the writings of individual collectors. Known as Hadith, this vast literature is the basis of Sunna. Literally Al-Hadith is any narrative, the root word being Hadatha (which means, he narrated). In its special meaning, it is the chronicle of the doings (Fil), Sayings (Qawl) and unspoken approval (Taqrir) of the Prophet which are recorded by his companions.

The Hadith must be genuine, its genuineness is ascertained if the Isnad or the Chain of Narrators is traced without any break from the last to the first narrator. The transmitters must also be true and reliable persons with sharp memory. If Isnad is established, Matn, the text of the Hadith is generally accepted without scrutiny. In the early period of Islam, it was easy to collect some three to five hundred thousand Hadith with little efforts. Most of them were, on close scrutiny by the learned found to be fakes; some others were imitations; few were half truths, and only very few indeed were genuine and sound.

First reliable and sincere attempt to compile Hadith was made by Mohammed Ismael Bukhari (A.H. 194 - 256) popularly known as *Bukhari*. He was so sincere a compiler of Hadith that he never recorded a Tradition without offering a two rakat worship. Labouring hard for 16 years and travelling from place to place, he had selected some 9882 traditions out of 600,000 he had collected and subjected to close scrutiny. Of the 9882 approved traditions, he held only 2623 as genuine, authentic and as of undisputed authority. It is surprising to know that Imam Bukhari acknowledges only 2,000 as reliable transmitters out of 40,000 persons. It is no doubt if his book (Jami'al-Sahih) is held in high esteem. The two best commentaries of Jami are the Umdat Al-Qari of Al-Ayni (d. 1451) and the Irshad Al-Sari of Al-Qastallani (d. 1517). Imam Bukhari lived in a mosque and died at the age of 64 in the year 872. Equally important is the Sahih of Imam Muslim ibn Hallaj (A.H. 204 - 261) who had scrutinised about 300,000 traditions. His book has 7275 traditions of which 4000 are approved to be genuine. He died because of over eating dates given to him by his friends while he was busy searching for a tradition in his house. The work involved was so serious to him that the learned scholar forgot the quantity of dates he had consumed.

The other important collectors of Hadith are.

1. Abu Daud Sajistani (A.H. 202 - 275). His book Sunan Abu Daud contains 4008 Traditions selected from 500,000. 2 Abu Isa Mohammed Tirmidhi popularly known as Tirmidhi (A.H. 209 - 279). He was the disciple of Bukhari and Abu Daud. His work was entitled Jami-i-Tirmidhi. 3. Abu Abdul Rahman Ahmed Nasai or simply Nasai (A.H. 303). He was beaten by the people of Damascus and subsequently succumbed to the injuries in A.D. 915. The book which was complied was Sunan-i-Nasai, 4. Ibn Maja (A.H. 293). His work is so important a book combined with the two Sahih of Bukhari and Muslim, the four Sunan (Collection)

of Abu Daud, Tirmidhi, Nasai and Ibn Maja form the great Six Books. To these works are sometimes added the Sunan of Moatta Imam Malik (A.H. 95 - 179) and the Sunan of Darimi. Coming to later years Baghawi (A.D. 1117) compiled a book (Maabih Al-Sunna) classifying the Traditions into Sound (Sahih), Fair (Hasan) and Rare (Gharib). He approved all the traditions in the two Sahih Books of Bukhari and Muslim as sound. After close scrutiny of the four Sunan Books, he had classified them into Hasan (Fair) and Gharib (Rare) Traditions. It was revised by Al-Tabriz and published as Mishkat al-Masabih. Other noteworthy books published recently are Kitab al-Arbain of Al-Nawawi (d. 1278) and the Jami Al-Saghir of Al-Suyuti (d. 1505).

Sunna combined with the Sira (that is the Biographical sketch of the Prophet with particular reference to his actions to a particular problem) and the study of Adab literature (enumeration of good manners) are studied by the Muslims for good conduct.

We observe that the Prophet had given utmost importance to prayer. Islam enjoins five ritual and innumerable superoragatory prayers. It is to be mentioned that even the number of ritual worship is fixed, based on Traditional literature, although here and there in Al-Quran references occur. Similarly, the Prophet had eulogised virtues and condemned vices. Seekers of knowledge were respected as the real soldiers of religion. One of his Sayings is that,"Pen is mightier than sword". He abhorred everything ugly and untidy, he taught his followers the importance of ritual purity before prayer. "Ablution is half of faith and the key of prayer," was his another great Saying. Minute regulations are prescribed for observing purification before prayer. The Prophet on another occasion said: Of all the things which can remove impurities from human beings, water is the best. Allah has created water clean. That quantity of water which can fill two large jars (Qull, about 266 litres) is supposed to be pure, if there is no change in colour, taste and odour. Generally, all water which are safe to drink can be used for ablution also. However, water is so important a necessity for a Muslim, without it, he is virtually lost. Water is everything for him. For his ablution before 5-time a day ritual worships, cleaning after urination, to remove legal impurities as in coitus, menstruation etc. water is a must even though Tayammum, cleaning by proxy with clean dust is permitted for ablution.

Prophet of Islam was a model par excellence.His disciples take pride in imitating him in every respect. Especially, when they are in doubt of their actions, they refer to the life of the Prophet, they see what he has done on similar occasions. His actions and sayings are considered as the best guidelines for all times to follow. The Prophet is reported to have visited the sick and commanded his followers to do the same. Himself seated on the bed of the sick man, he would lay his right hand on the sick man's body saying:

"Remove the ban Thou Lord of man!
O Healer, heal, relieve
There is no cure besides Thy cure
Help, Helper, we believe."

Cleanliness is next to Godliness. It is almost a religious duty for the Muslims to be clean physically. For this purpose the Prophet introduced ablution before every prayer. Now no ritual prayer is performed without ablution with clean water. The Prophet used to cleanse his teeth with a wooden tooth-brush. This he is reputed to have done in his last agonies when Abdul Rahman, brother of Aisha entered his apartment with a tooth-brush in his hand. The Prophet looked at it. Aisha who knew his liking for tooth brushes took it from him, chewed it in her mouth to make it more pliable and soft and gave it to the Prophet. With it, he cleansed his teeth and before long he died lying in the bosom of his wife. Such was the great lesson of physical purity he taught to his followers that they too give considerable importance to it.

The Prophet used to recite the Quran distinctly and clearly, stopping at times and raising his voice at the appropriate words. To give more emphasis, he pairs his fingers, or raises or lowers his voice. On Id al Fitr, he used to go round the congregation exhorting them to give alms. He used to tell the same thing to women who were there in the congregation. Prophet of Islam was very pleased to hear others reciting Al-Quran especially those who had a good, sonorous voice. Sometimes tears flowed from his eyes. Such was his feeling. Friday used to be a busy day for the Prophet, he used to cleanse his clothes himself and take bath before proceeding to Mosque. There he never waited for others to greet him. He was the first to greet the congregation.

It is reported that the Prophet once said,"There are three things, no one of which is good—Quick Temper (Al-Tayaratu), Suspicion (Al-Zannu) and Envy (Al-Hasad). When someone asked, "And what is the way of escape from these things?" Thereupon he said, "When you are in temper do not answer, when you only suspect, do not be certain, and when you feel envy, do not become covetous." Similarly he had said to his companions that the worst men are those who divulge slanderous news. An oft quoted saying of the Prophet is, "Of the things which are lawful, the most hateful to God is divorce." But the meaning of this Tradition as several others is lost to the Faithfuls. Similarly the Quranic injunction to pronounce the divorce formula separately on three occasions and the procedure of remarrying divorced women (Halalah) are now conveniently dispensed with. Now many marry, divorce and marry again making the religious law a mockery.

Some of the Sayings of the Holy Prophet

- Seek ye knowledge even (as far as) China.
- The acquisition of knowledge is incumbent upon every Muslim, male and female.
- Paradise is at the feet of thy mother.
- The ink of the scholar is more holy than the blood of the martyr.
- Give the labourer his wage before his perspiration dries.
- He is not one of us who sleeps while his neighbour is hungry.
- The best of God's subjects in the eyes of God is one of most use to His servants.
- When one of you undertakes a certain duty, one should bring it to perfection.
- Actions will be judged according to intentions.
- Do not speak ill of the dead.
- Be merciful to people on earth. You will be entitled for the Mercy of Him who is in the heaven.
- Love of this world is the root cause of all sins.
- Fight your passions you gain control of yourself.
- The best of wisdom is the fear of God.
- The learned are the heirs of the Prophets.
- Seeking knowledge is mandatory for every Muslim.
- The best of you is the best to his family.
- Your body has a right upon you.
- Beg not anything from the people.
- A man hasn't earned better income than that which is from his own labour.
- Your own self has a right upon you.
- The most perfect Believers are the best in conduct and the best of you are best to their wives.
- The hand that is above is better than the hand that is below.
- It is generous who is good to women and it is wicked who insults them.

Before passing on to the religious duties prescribed to the Muslims, we shall now turn to the Economic Principles of Islam which too emanate from the Divine Law.

ECONOMIC PRINCIPLES OF ISLAM

Based on Divine Law, Islam has laid down a detailed economic system free from any exploitation. Before Allah, all are equal. Its chief objective is the creation of a society in which each stands for all and all for each. Islam recognises lawful earnings of income and prescribes how to spend it. Neither be a miser nor a spendthrift. In either case, it is a sin. "Be neither miserly nor prodigal, for then ye should either be prepared or be reduced to penury." (Sura XVII. The Night Journey)

Islam rightly lays great stress on free market economy and guarantees ample chances for individual earnings on permissible legal means. God created the earth and everything contained in it for the use of His creation, to all mankind, to all birds and beasts. Every human being has equal right for everything provided by God. Thus, one's right to the extent of his needs for air, sunlight, water from open sea and big rivers, game birds and beasts from forests is recognised. At the same time it condemns felling fruit bearing trees, keeping land unutilised for a long time. The land belongs to the tillers. It is recorded on the authority of Hadhrat Salem ibn Abdullah Zahari that once Hadhrat Umar declared any desert plot of land will be the property of anyone who brings it on use and anyone who does not make use of it for three years will have no right on it whatsoever. The maximum period the land can be left unused is three years. If on the fourth year if any one uses it, the property belongs to the actual user and not the former who loses his right of ownership.

One of the basic belief of Islam is that human nature differs. One may be more intelligent with a good physique and be a hard worker. Another may be an idiot or lazy and unintelligent. Even though Islam recognises the right to live for both these types of men, it did not disapprove the right of the former to profit himself because of his hard work. In other words, Islam recognises social justice not at the cost of individual ownership, income or earning. Whoever owns a land fully, keeps it lawfully is the rightful owner of his property. Shariah or the Islamic Legal System protects the rights of individual.

But Islam has a realistic answer without tears to the great problem of redistribution of income. It is Zakat, the compulsory payment of legal alms, and the voluntary payment of charity to the poor and the needy. It is so important a virtue, Zakat is one of the five pillars of Islam incumbent on every Muslim. Elaborate details are given in Al-Quran and Sunna for its collection and distribution which is given in Chapter 4. Al-Quran has several passages on alms-giving. The Script also clearly names the persons who are eligible to receive charity which debars all those who are well off. Eligibility to receive charity is restricted to the poor, the orphans, the needy and indigent and for the release of captives and for the benefit of wayfarers.

Zakat is a tax without tears. It is to be paid at the rate of $2^1/2\%$ of one's wealth in possession for one full year and invested capital, 5% to 10% on agricultural produce and 20% on mineral products.

With a view to minimise the concentration of wealth to few hands, Islam disfavours hoarding and monopoly. "Proclaim a woeful punishment to those that hoard up gold and silver and do not spend it in Allah's cause. The day will surely come when their treasures shall be heated in the fire of Hell, and their foreheads, sides and backs branded with them." (Sura 9:34) More can be read in Sura 104:1 and Sura 70. Hell fire shall drag him (the hoarder) by the scalp who amassed riches and covetously hoarded them. Al-Quran reprimands those who display their riches. "Do not exult in your riches; Allah does not love the exultant." (Sura 28) Thus hoarding and display of riches discouraged, Islam adopts more stringent measures for the promotion of the economic welfare of the people at large. To bring about rapid circulation of income and wealth, Islam encourages expenditure and investment.

Islamic Law of Inheritance also is directed towards the distribution of the amassed wealth and property of the deceased person to many persons. In other words, the wealth of a person, on his death passes on to his near relatives, on whose absence, to distant relatives. If there is no distant relative, it goes to the state, that is the Muslim society. This is a diffusion of wealth and property as given in the Islamic Divine Law. Another virtue of Islamic Inheritance is that women too are eligible to inherit property along with men and have the full right to own and dispose it.

In Islam there are no privileged classes. Al-Quran warns the Muslims. "O true believers, verily many of the priests and monks defraud men of their possessions and obstruct them from the way of God." (Sura 9:33) In brief, the Divine Law guarantees equal status and opportunities to all.

In the social life, Islam had revolutionised an incomparable change in the annals of history. Firstly, Islam had united one of the most disorderly people to a mighty force. Having learnt a dictum from their master that a "Believer is one who does to others whatever he does to himself," the inhabitants of Arabia formed themselves into a Community of Believers, who had never forsaken this unity in spite of diversity of languages, culture and nationality that separated them. When Islam spread with rapid speed beyond the borders of Arabia, this Unity was a binding force. The Muslims, wherever they were, ate from the same plate, slept under the same tent, and fought together and won many decisive battles. Within a few years of its establishment, Islam had its Houses of Worship in many countries of the world. A major contribution of Islam is the abolition of sectarian and racial prejudices. Probably, it is the first time in the history of mankind that equality is maintained in Prayer. Before God all Muslims stand shoulder to shoulder in obedience, in perfect silence engrossed in praising Him. To perpetuate this Brotherhood and Oneness among themselves, certain duties (Farz Kifai) are prescribed. The important duties under this category are to return a salutation, visit the sick and disabled persons, follow a bier, accept invitation for food, reply to a sneezing, give advice when asked for, assist a person in his duties, and to help Muslims in distress. It is praiseworthy if all the members do it. Unless at least one for every ten citizens perform this, the entire community is blameworthy.

Another immediate achievement of Islam is the abolition of all intermediaries between God and man. Throughout the Islamic world, there is no priesthood, nor any established class of people who live on the ignorance of men. Thus in Islam, a man's approach to his Creator is direct and sincere.

Morality and piety are one and the same in Islam. A combination of these made the Muslims virtuous and noble, and they were received as the real saviours by many of their neighbouring countries. Being morally strong, they won the confidence of the vanquished and being pious, they gained them for their faith.

Politically, Islamic movement was to establish democracy as against the mercantile oligarchy. It aims at the moulding of an orderly society under definite rule from a nation of vagabonds who never respected any law.

Above all, Islam's simplicity is its greatest asset. Its chief dogma probably the simplest—Oneness of God and that Muhammad is His Rasul—is easy to understand and recite. A sincere belief of this formula and recitation make one converted to the Community of Believers. Even the unlettered from the wide desert had accepted this formula without any reservation, and many early converts attained freedom too by uttering the Islamic dogma. As Muslims, they enjoyed equal rights with their masters. All the successors to the Prophet, even though they were the temporal as well as the spiritual heads were as simple as the common man in the street. This simplicity at the height of glory had won many followers and probably was the chief reason of its rapid success.

3. IMAN OR FAITH

Islam is a religion of Faith (Iman) and Practices (Amal). Faith is the acceptance and acknowledgement that something is true. Knowing a thing or mere knowledge (Ma'rifa) of a thing does not constitute Faith. But knowing a thing, accepting it and confessing it to make it binding is the real test of having Faith. In the Wasiyat Abi Hanifa, Faith is defined as consists of confessing with tongue, believing with the mind and knowing with the heart[1]. The Orthodox define Faith as acceptance of belief (Tasdiq), confession of it (Iqrar) and action (Amal). So according to this, acceptance and confession of belief followed by good work and conduct alone make one a true Believer. Obviously, a person who does good work without acceptance of belief and confession of it by word of mouth is a hypocrite (Monafiq). A person who has faith in the Islamic dogma, as in these six articles of belief, is a Mu'min. Those who associate anything with God are Mushrikin, i.e., Associates. On the contrary, a person who performs the ritual duties is a Muslim. So all Mu'min need not necessarily be Muslims, but all Muslims must be Mu'min for the ritual duties confirm the Islamic articles of belief. A hypocrite has three distinct qualities. They are lying, breaking promises and cheating. (Bukhari, Hadith Narrator Abu Huraira, a trusted Companion of Prophet). Kafir is one who had Kufr, that is unbelief. Those who are not believers are Infidels (Kafir). Anyone who omits to perform the prayer voluntarily is a Kafir. On the contrary, Mushrikin is a polytheist or one who believes in more than one god or shirk. This is opposed to a Monafiq who is hypocrite, that is one who has no Faith but has a good conduct and does good works.

Faith consists of the following six articles of belief:-

1. The Oneness of Allah (Tawhid)
2. Al-Malaikah (the Angels)
3. Al-Kutub (the Inspired Book)
4. Ar-Rasul (the Messenger)

---

[1] Requoted from the Muslim Creed. A Wensick Cambridge U. Press, London 1932, p. 125. Similarly in The Faith Akbar II (Art. 18) it is given "Faith consists in confessing and believing. "The Faithful are equal in faith and in the confession of the Unity of Allah they are different in degree of superiority regarding works". Ibid p. 194.

5. Al-Yaumul-Akhir (the last Day)
6. Al-Qudar (the Decree of God and Predestination)

Known as Arkanual-Iman or the Pillars of Faith, the six articles of Belief form the chief plank on which the great edifice of Islam is built. Ali the son of Abu Talib and the fourth Caliph narrates that "the Messenger of Allah said that no one can be called a believer unless he believes in four (things) to bear witness that there is no god but Allah and that I, Muhammad, am the Messenger of Allah, who sent me with truth, and to believe in death, and to believe in resurrection after death, and to believe in predestination." (Tirmidhi)[2]

Articles of beliefs occur in many places in Quran. In Sura II: 285, a summary is given.

> *"Each one believeth in Allah and His angels*
> *and His Scriptures and His Messengers*
> *We make no distinction between any of His messengers----"*

> Again it occurs in Sura IV: 136
> *"O ye who believe! Believe in Allah and His*
> *messenger and the Scripture which He hath*
> *revealed unto His messenger, and the Scripture*
> *which He revealed aforetime. Whoso believeth*
> *in Allah and His angels and His Scriptures and*
> *His messengers and the Last Day, he verily hath*
> *wandered far astray."*

Even though, the Quran contains only brief expressions of Islamic beliefs, Traditions and its vast literature serve as a compendium of creed.

One of the fundamental Quranic preachings is that belief and good works save men from the torments of hell, for it states "Lo! those who believe and do good works, there are the Gardens of Paradise for welcome." (Sura XVIII: 108) Imam Bukhari[3] and Imam Muslim [3] have passed as genuine the following Hadith which states that faith and faith alone will save men from the torments of hell. It is related from Ubada ibn As-Samit that,"the Apostle of God said,'whoever bears witness that there is no god but Allah alone, and that He has no partner, and that Muhammad is His Servant and His Apostle and that Jesus is the ser-

---

2. The English Translation of the Holy Traditions Vol, I by M.M. Ilahi, Lahore 1st Ed, 1932. p. 19.

3. First two and the most reliable of the Six famous Compilers of Hadith.

vant of God and His Apostle and the son of His handmaid and His word which He cast into Mary and a spirit from Him, and (bears witness) that heaven and hell are true, God will take him into paradise in spite of what his works may have been.' [4]" Moaz son of Jabal Ansari narrates that the Messenger of Allah said that whose last words would be 'there is no god but Allah', he will enter the paradise (Abu Dawud)[5]. In the Hadith literature also Faith stands a shade ahead to work. Imam Bukhari has recorded a Tradition on the basis of oral narration of Abu Sa'id Khudri, a companion of the Prophet that the Prophet had said: "After the just were admitted to the Paradise and unjust had entered the hell, Allah will say,'let those who have Iman even to the size of a mustard seed come out.' They blackened to a deep dark colour come out and enter into a river (of pure rain water or of some other water). Thus purified in it, they would sprout into a new figure like a seed on the banks of a river germinate into a plant. Did you not see green plants so sprout on the banks of river.'' The Traditionalist rely and cite a story wherein the Prophet had sent Abu Huraira[6] with his shoes as a symbol of his authority to declare that whoever bears witness from the heart that there is no god but Allah to him will be the good tidings of heaven. Umar[7] was the first to meet Abu Huraira to whom the latter unhesitatingly declared the importance of Faith over work.. It so annoyed Umar that he struck Abu Huraira on his breast. Then Umar went to the Prophet and asked whether it was true that he sent Abu Huraira with such and such a declaration. Having heard an affirmative reply from the Prophet, Umar said, "If it so, men will depend upon Faith alone. Better, leave them alone." Agreeing with Umar, the Apostle said, "Leave them alone." This leads us to the conclusion that eventhough Faith is sufficient for salvation, work must not be neglected. This led the orthodox to the belief that Faith never decreases nor increases and Muslim always remains a Muslim whatsoever sin he may commit. The Kharijites, a sect of the Muslims while rejecting it hold the opinion that Muslims on account of grave sins lose the faith and no longer belong to the community. In other words great sinners are not 'Faithful'. Or Faithful could never do great sins.

---

[4]Selection from Muhammedan Traditions by Rev. W. Goldsack. p. 3.

[5]The English Translation of the Holy Traditions. Vol. 1 by M. M. Illahi (Lahore) p. 4.

[6]A Companion of the Prophet.

[7]The Second Caliph.

Faith consists in word (Qawl) and in work (Amal) and that it increases and decreases.[8] Al-Quran also affirms that Faith increases.[9] The sign of having Faith is one doing good work. Works are acts of obedience and so good works for self, family, neighbours and for the humanity as a whole are the best sign having Faith. Good works in Islam include helping and kind words, removal of nuisance from roads, and even one's modesty and pious talks. The Prophet said, "He who is not true to his trust has no faith, and he who does not keep his promise has no religion." In answer to a query by a person who had asked the Prophet about the best of the Islamic works, he said, "Giving food to others and greeting known and unknown person with 'Salam' (are the best works) " (Bukhari from Abdulla ibn Amr). Abdul-Kahir Al-Baghdadi in his famous book, Kitab Usul al-Din (p. 249) says that "Faith consists of the sum total of good works (Ta'at), obligatory as well as supererogatory. It has three stages. In the first of these the Faithful emerges from unbelief and is delivered from eternal punishment, provided that he dies in this faith. It consists in knowledge concerning Allah, His books, His apostles, the decree for good and for evil; and further in acknowledging the eternal qualities of Allah, in rejecting anthropomorphism and nihilism, in admitting the possibility of seeing Him, and in believing all other authoritative traditions which are entirely trustworthy. The second stage renders the Faithful an irreproachable Muslim, keeps away from him the qualification of fasiq, and preserves him from the fire. It consists in performing obligatory works and in avoiding mortal sins. The third stage brings the Faithful to the highest class which contains those who will enter Paradise without being called to account. It consists in performing obligatory as well as supererogatory works, and in avoiding all kinds of sins."[10]

The orthodox Muslims hold the view that Faith neither increase nor decrease, that is there is no degree in Faith. No Muslim, on any ground, is exempted from Faith. On the contrary, on certain strong rea-

---

[8] Al-Ashari. Born at al-Basra in A.H. 260 and died after A.H. 320. He upheld the 7 rational qualities (Sifat Aqliya) of God - Life, Knowledge, Power, Will, Hearing, Seeing, and Speech. His system now known as Asharite. Ibn Maja also holds the same view. Al-Bukhari also declares in his Iman that Faith will increase and decrease. The Quranic passage occurs in Sura XLVIII:4, Sura LXXIV:31, Sura III:167, Sura XXXIII:22 and Sura XLVII:19.

[9] Sura IX:124 (Repentance).

[10] The Muslim Creed, A.J. Wensinck. p. 134.

sons even the performance of the most important religious duties—Salat, Saum, Zakat and Haj can be postponed. For example, women in menstruation need not perform Salat. Sick persons and suckling mothers are exempted from fasting. Almsgiving is not compulsory for the poor who have no means or income. Lastly, Pilgrimage is obligatory only for those who are capable of meeting the expenses for the journey.

This leads us to the difference between a Muslim and a Mu'min. The words at the outset appear to be complimentary and interchangeable but in the strict sense, they denote two different stages. A Mu'min is a Muslim. He must have Faith (Iman) and must do good work. So, obviously a person who does noble work without faith is not a Mu'min. By virtue of his deeds, he is a Muslim.

This further leads us to the problem that human beings cannot say whether a person is a Mu'min or not as we are incapable of judging the Faith. After all Faith is inner. Good works without Faith have no meaning and will not save one from the punishment (Sura XVIII:102-107). Al-Quran states, "Shall we inform you who will be the greatest losers by their works? Those whose efforts goeth astray in the life of the world, and yet they reckon that they do good work. Those are they who disbelieve in the revelations of their Lord and in the meeting with Him. Therefore their works are vain, and on the Day of Resurrection We assign no weight to them " (Sura XVIII. 102-107).

Then, what about a person who has Faith, commits a great sin. The orthodox Muslims say that if such a believer (since he has Faith) dies unrepentant, he will be punished for the sin in hell and later, will be admitted to Paradise. To them Hell is something like a Purgatory. Or God may forgive him even without repentance. This view is not shared by all sects of Islam. For example, Kharijites held the extreme view. An unrepentant sinner even though has confessed his Faith ceases to be a Muslim, and he will remain in hell for ever. So Kharijites, contrary to the belief of the orthodox, believed that Faith increases and decreases.[11] For a grave sinner, if unrepentant, it decreases even to nil and he ceases to be a Muslim. Asuming the view that the man and

---

[11] In the Wasiyat Abi Hanifa it is said that "Faith is not liable to increase; or decrease. For its decrease can only be conceived of in connection with increase of unbelief; and its increase can only be conceived of in connection with decrease of unbelief; This would imply that one individual should be faithful and infidel at the same time, and how is this possible?" p. 125.

man alone is the author of his acts, Mutazilites, a still later sect of Islam held a middle position. They said that the sinners will be in an intermediate state (Manzila Bain Al-Mamzilatain).

I. BELIEF IN ALLAH

The Quranic God is Allah, a title difficult to find expression in any other language. It is a title of its own. The term consists of two arabic syllable, Alif and Hā connected by two 'Lam'. The interpretation is that the first syllable 'Alif' refers to the world and the life in this world, and the second syllable Hā indicates the life beyond. Brackctted in between these two realities—life in this world and the life in the other world—is the two 'Lams'. They obviously indicate death and resurrection, the other two realities. The title as a whole stands for the present life, death and resurrection, and a future life. Its symbolical representation indicates serenity, majesty and mystery. The horizontal line of the first syllable (Alif) refers to serenity, the vertical line of Lam to majesty, and the final circle, the mystery. However for general purposes, the name is translated as "the One Supreme Deity" or simply "God". Allah is the eternal Being. The origin of the word is disputed by the doctors of Islam. It is probable that Allah is Al plus Ilah shortened Allah meaning the God. Or, it is Al and Lah combined to form Allah (the Secret One) Allah Ta'la is meant 'The Most High God'.

In Al-Quran it is said that "if all the trees in the earth were pens, and the sea with seven more seas to replenish it, were ink, the writing of Allah's words could never be finished. Mighty is Allah and wise" (Sura 31. Luqman). The other titles of Allah are called the Ismu'z Zat. His attributes form the excellent names of God. (Sura 7) The Traditions record the following ninety-nine names, Asma'ul-Husna.[12]

---

[12] Sura 7

"Most excellent are the names of Allah. Call on Him by His names and keep away from those that pervert them. They shall be punished for their misdeeds."

It is said Walid ibn Mughaira had scoffed at Muhammad when he gave the title Al Rahman (The Merciful) to God. Walid said, he knew nothing about that title except a man having that name in Yamama. The Meccans had gods whose names derived from divine qualities, viz, Allat from Allah, Al Uzza from Al Aziz (the mighty) and Manat from Al Mannan (The Bountiful). Hence, he refused to recognise the title Al Rahman and other names. God warns those liers thus:

"Those who devise lies against our signs we will suffer them to fall gradually into ruin, by a method which they know not." (Sura VII)

1.	Al - Rahman	=	The Merciful
2.	Ar - Rahim	=	The Compassionate
3.	Al - Malik	=	The King
4.	Al - Quddus	=	The Holy
5.	As - Salam	=	The Peace
6.	Al - Mu'min	=	The Faithful
7.	Al - Muhaimin	=	The Protector
8.	Al - Aziz	=	The Mighty
9.	Al - Jabbar	=	The Repairer
10.	Al - Mutakabbir	=	The Great
11.	Al - Khaliq	=	The Creator
12.	Al - Bari	=	The Maker
13.	Al - Musawwir	=	The Fashioner
14.	Al - Ghaffar	=	The Forgiver
15.	Al - Qahhar	=	The Dominant
16.	Al - Wahhab	=	The Bestower
17.	Al - Razzaq	=	The Provider
18.	Al - Fattah	=	The Opener
19.	Al - Alim	=	The Knower
20.	Al - Qabiz	=	The Restrainer
21.	Al - Basit	=	The Spreader
22.	Al - Khafiz	=	The Abaser
23.	Ar - Rafi	=	The Exalter
24.	Al - Mu'izz	=	The Honourer
25.	Al - Muzil	=	The Destroyer
26.	As - Sami	=	The Hearer
27.	Al - Basir	=	The Seer
28.	Al - Hakim	=	The Ruler
29.	Al - Adl	=	The Just
30.	Al - Latif	=	The Subtle
31.	Al - Khabir	=	The Aware
32.	Al - Halim	=	The Clement
33.	Al - Azim	=	The Grand
34.	Al - Ghafur	=	The Forgiving
35.	Ash - Shakur	=	The Grateful
36.	Al - Ali	=	The Exalted
37.	Al - Kabir	=	The Great
38.	Al - Hafiz	=	The Guardian
39.	Al - Muqit	=	The Strengthener
40.	Al - Hasib	=	The Reckoner

41.	Al - Jalil	=	The Majestic
42.	Al - Karim	=	The Generous
43.	Al - Raqib	=	The Watcher
44.	Al - Mujib	=	The Approver
45.	Al - Wasi	=	The Comprehensive
46.	Al - Hakeem (Al-Hakim)	=	The Wise
47.	Al - Wadud	=	The Loving
48.	Al - Majeed	=	The Glorious
49.	Al - Bais	=	The Raiser
50.	Ash - Shahid	=	The Witness
51.	Al - Haqq	=	The Truth
52.	Al - Wakil	=	The Advocate
53.	Al - Qawi	=	The Strong
54.	Al - Matin	=	The Firm
55.	Al - Wali	=	The Patron
56.	Al - Hamid	=	The Laudable
57.	Al - Muhsi	=	The Counter
58.	Al - Mubdi	=	The Beginner
59.	Al - Mu'id	=	The Restorer
60.	Al - Muhyi	=	The Quickner
61.	Al - Mumit	=	The Killer
62.	Al - Haiy	=	The Living
63.	Al - Qaiyum	=	The Subsisting
64.	Al - Wajid	=	The Finder
65.	Al - Majid	=	The Glorious
66.	Al - Wahid	=	The One
67.	Al - Samad	=	The Eternal
68.	Al - Qadir	=	The Powerful
69.	Al - Muqtadir	=	The Preventing
70.	Al - Muqaddim	=	The Bringer Forward
71.	Al - Mu'akhkhir	=	The Deferrer
72.	Al - Awwal	=	The First
73.	Al - Akhir	=	The Last
74.	Az - Zahir	=	The Evident
75.	Al - Batin	=	The Hidden
76.	Al - Wali	=	The Governor
77.	Al - Muta'ali	=	The Exalted
78.	Al - Barr	=	The Righteous
79.	Al - Tauwab	=	The Accepter of Repentance

80.	Al - Muntaqim	=	The Avenger
81.	Al - Afuw	=	The Pardoner
82.	Ar - Ra'uf	=	The Kind
83.	Maliku'l-Mulk	=	The Ruler of the Kingdom
84.	Zu'l-Jalali Wa'l Ikram	=	The Lord of Majesty and Liberality
85.	Al -Muqsit	=	The Equitable
86.	Al - Jami	=	The Collector
87.	Al - Ghani	=	The Independent
88.	Al - Mughni	=	The Enricher
89.	Al - Mu'ti	=	The Giver
90.	Al - Mani	=	The Withholder
91.	Az - Zarr	=	The Distresser
92.	An - Nafi	=	The Profiter
93.	An - Nur	=	The Light
94.	Al - Hadi	=	The Guide
95.	Al - Badi	=	The Incomparable
96.	Al - Baqi	=	The Enduring
97.	Al - Waris	=	The Inheritor
98.	Ar - Rashid	=	The Director
99.	As - Sabur	=	The Patient.

Adding the essential name of God, Allah (Ismu'z Zat), The list has 100 names.

However, Religious Scholars believe, Allah has 3,000 names--1000 each are known to angels and Prophets, 300 each occur in Old Testament (Torah), Psalms (Zabour) and New Testament and 99 in Al-Quran making a total of 2,999. The last name is undisclosed and is the Greatest Name of Allah or Ism Allah al-Azam which is believed containing in Al-Quran but hidden and the reciters of the Sacred Text read the name without knowing it. All His Names are great indeed and those who repeat it many times are supposed to become obsessed by the particular attributes of God. To become rich some pious people repeat Yadhul Jalal - Wal - Ikram (The Lord of Majesty and Bounty). He who repeats Ya - Akhir (The Last) will lead a good life and will have a good end, and who repeats Ya - Aziz forty times after each Fajr Prayer for forty days will be self sufficient. Similarly, if one repeats Ya Mutakabbir before intercourse with his wife, Allah will bless him with a righteous child. If a farmer writes the Name Al-Halim, i.e., The

Forbearing One and puts it in to the field, he can expect a rich harvest. The better of all is to repeat the Islamic Creed La Ilaha Illa Allah Muhammad An Rasulullah (There is no god but Allah and Muhammad in His Messenger).

Some of God's titles depict His glorious attributes (Asma-ul Jalaliya) and others, the terrible attributes (Asmaul Jamaliya)[1]. Ar-Rahman (the merciful), Ar-Raheem (the Compassionate), As-Salam (the Peace), Al-Ghaffar (the Foregiver), Al-Aziz (the Preserver), Al-Karim (the Bountiful) etc. are the Glorious names; and Al-Hathim (the Mighty), Al-kahhar (the Dominant), Al-Aziz (the Strong), Al-Kawi (the Almighty), Al-Mateen (the Firm), Al-Muktadir (the All-Powerful), Al-Muntakim (the Avenger) are His Terrible Names. God has seven principal names called Ayimmatul Asma. They are

Al-Hayy (the Living)
Al-Alim (the Knowing)
Al-Murid (the Purpose)
Al-Qadir (the Powerful)
Al-Sami (the Hearer)
Al-Basir (the Seer)
Al-Mutakallim (the Speaker)

The essential dogma of Islam is Tawhid or belief in the Oneness of God, God is one and ONE only. There is no other reality, other than God. He is eternal and indivisible. It is condensed in a single phrase: La Ilah Illallah. The elements of the Absolute Unity of God even though occurs throughout Quran, they are predominant in Sura II. 256, Sura XXVII. 26, and Sura CXII. Sura XXVIII. 88 states the Unity of God precisely thus: "And cry not unto any other god along with Allah. There is no God save him. Everything will perish save His countenance. His is the command, and unto Him ye will be brought back"

Again in Sura CXII, it is given as follows:

"Say! He is Allah, the One!
Allah, the eternity, Besought of all!
He begetteth not nor was begotten.
And there is none comparable unto Him."

God has absolutely no Partner and that no one is equal or rival to Him. He has no associate, nor sharer. He has taken no wife to Him,

---

[1]The Theology of Unity by Muhammad Abdu, p. 29. London, 1966.

nor child. He has no beginning, not ending. Without having no form, or shape, He is colourless. He is the only Creator and Restorer of all things in the world and heavens. He is powerful, mighty, omnipresent, omnipotent and omniscient. He is the Hearer of everything and Seer of all things. He has full knowledge of all things of the past, present and future, and knows all secrets however small it may be. These attributes are emanations of the Essence of God (Dhat) and not to be understood independently of the Essence of God. Allah willed that nothing could happen without His Will, Knowledge, Decision, and Decree. He is the most Gracious. He rewards the good actions twice. He punishes the sinners by justice. He forgives by grace.

Islam is the religion of Absolute. Allah is the ony Creator and the Sustainer. He has created eveything by saying "KUN" or 'BE' (Sura XVI. 40). God has created the Universe in six days[1]—first two days for the heavens and the earth and during the remaining four days, He has filled the space with smoke and then He has created water, earth, mountains and then on a Friday, Adam was created. He created man in His own image, angels from light (Nur) and jins from fire (Nar) so that they might obediently serve Him. God in Islam is the Universal God of Love. In Sura An-Nar (Sura CXIV) God is addressed as Lord of Mankind (Rabbin-Nas), King of mankind (Ilah i Nas). He is the Most, Beneficent (Ar-Rahman) and the Most Merciful (Ar-Raheem). He is the Lord of the Universe (Rabbil-Alameen) (Sura I. 1,2,3.) He decides everything according to His incalculable Will. To know His Will by His creatures, He caused a Rasul (Messenger) to arise from any nation He chooses. Many are the Rasul who preached on the earth, last in the series is Muhammad who is the greatest of them all and the Last (Seal of the Prophet). All the Prophets preached the Unity of God, but the people continued to be hostile to the true religion, followed the polytheism and idolatry of their ancestors. One day the whole world, men, birds, trees, everything will be caused to die, and caused to live again for the Final Judgement. The Just will be separated from the Unjust, who will find their permanent abodes in the Garden of Paradise, and the Unjust will fall into the Hell. That is the ever lasting reward and punishment.

God is the Hearer, the Seer (Sura II. 233, 237, XXIV. 28). He knows everything but His hearing is different from that of the created things. His seeing does not have the qualities of created things. That is His

---

[1]Sura LVII. 4, Sura XLI. 9. 10.

Seeing is not with the eyeball as the creatures see. Nor His hearing through the ears. His knowledge is not through the brain. Nor does he hold or seize with the help of limbs and hands.

God has many negative qualities also. There is no multiplicity in God, nor weakness in Him. He has no consort. He is not lacking in will and choice. He is not ignorant. There is no death for Him. He is not deaf, dumb or weak.

Some centuries later, the doctrine of Absolute Unity was put into severe test by the Absolute Oneness (Tawhid) of Allah by Djahm Ibn Safwan.[1] His thoughts were: Allah is the only Creator and Eternal; Quran like Paradise and Hell, is not uncreated. If it is uncreated and eternal, so argued the learned scholar, it amounts to another eternal and uncreated thing beside God. That shows multiplicity of Absolute Unity which is impossible. So Quran must be created. This thought at last drove him to the created worlds of Paradise and Hell, which made him to deny eternal reward and punishment as all the created things including Paradise and Hell would vanish. And God alone will remain as before the creation.

As a matter of fact, belief in God has a much wider outlook. There is a Tradition approved by the five authentic Hadith Collectors as sound running like this: Abu Huraira has narrated that 'The Messenger of Allah said that there are 70 and more branches of belief (in Allah), and modesty is one of the branches of belief (in Allah)'. As a rejoinder, it is recorded that the best of the branches is to believe that 'there is no god but Allah,' and least of them is to remove nuisance from the path. This shows the belief in Allah should be accompanied by good works. A mere belief in God has no meaning if the believer continues to be unjust, or indulges in wickedness. Hospitality, politeness, good manners, all are good works.

In Sura IV. 36, it is given "Show kindness unto parents, and unto near kindred, and orphans, and the needy, and unto the neighbour who is of kin (unto you) and the neighbour who is not of kin, and the fellow-traveller and the wayfarer and (the slaves) whom your right hands possess. Lo! Allah loveth not such as are proud and boastful."(Sura IV.36)

All these beliefs and several others of the orthodox Islam were not easily digestible to a few Muslims of the second and third centuries

---

[1]He was killed at Marw about the end of the reign of the Umayyads.

of the Hijrat.[1] They began reasoning everything, applying reasons to the dogma. Giving lead to this thinking was Wasil Ibn Ata. He thought that man and man alone is responsible for the actions he does, and not God. If God wills that such and such a person must do this or that act and punishing or rewarding him on this account has no meaning. It even amounts to injustice. Indeed many Muslims shared his thinking and they further argued that God is one and describing Him having various attributes makes him a separate Being. They rejected this multiplicity of God's attributes and all anthropomorphisms supposed to be in God. They also scoff at the idea that Believers could see God sitting in His Throne in Paradise, for God is unlimited. And so God would never sit in a place. Wasil Ibn Ata and his followers were called Mu't-azilites (Outgoers) and their doctrine was known as Mu'tazila (the Secession). Even though, they could hold ground for some time during the reign of Al-Mamun, everything was not lost to the Orthodoxy. They believed whatever given by the Traditionalists without asking how (Bila Kayfa).

The Essence of God (Dhat) and His attributes are not separate. They are one and the same. In fact His Attributes are the very Essence of God. Allah's sitting, seeing are His qualities.

II. BELIEF IN ANGELS OR MALAIKAH

Belief in angels is the second article of Faith. Angels are obedient servants of Allah and are believed to have been created from light (Nur). They are endowed with life, speech and reason but have no sex. They drink not; nor they eat. in Al-Quran, it is narrated how three angels, Gabriel, Michael and Israfil disguised as human beings visited Abraham with glad tidings of a son to him who immediately brought a roasted calf for them but they refused to eat because being angels, they need no food. (Sura II, 15 and 51). According to Abdul Muntaha, angels are "subtle bodies capable of assuming different forms. They are preserved from sin and they never transgress the commands of Allah". Probably they are innumerable, numberless. In the Traditional literature, it is said that the Prophet had seen in the Baitul Maamar (the counterpart of Mecca in heaven) seventy thousand angels entering daily

[1]The day of Prophet's emigration to Medina, Islamic Calendar reckons from this date.

and never returning when he was permitted to have a glimpse of heaven. Their only duty is to serve God faithfully. They were assigned different works. Some encircle the Throne of Allah, praising and prostrating before Him. Some others bear God's revelations and commands as Gabriel has brought Revelation to the Prophet Muhammad (PBUH). There are angels who console the Faithful (Sura XII. 30) and implore Allah's Forgiveness on their behalf (Sura XLII.3). One angel accomplishes the separation of soul from the body when men die, punishing the infidels was the chief duty of some others (Sura III.99, VI.93, VIII.52, XVI.30, XXXIV.35, XXV.24, XLVII.29). The other important duty of some specially favoured angels is to carry the Throne of God on the Day of Resurrection (Sura XXI.103 and XIX.1).

Four of them are Archangel (Karubiyin) for important assignments are given to them. They are Gabriel, Izrail, Azrafel and Michael. Gabriel is the medium of Revelation and is called the Ruh Al-Quds (Breath of Holiness). Muhammad (PBUH) received revelation through him. The belief is that Gabriel takes only one hour to descend from heaven to earth. He has not less than six hundred wings, each of them is so strong to lift mountain, however great it may be. It is further believed that Gabriel will hold the Balance (the Ma'zan) whose one scale will hang in paradise and the other, in Hell on the Judgement Day. (Sura II.91 and 254, LXVI.4, V.109, XVI.104, XIX.17, XXVI. 193-5, LIII.5-18). Izrail is the Malakul Maut or the Angel of Death who comes to the man at the hour of death to receive his soul (Sura XXXIII.11).

There is a tradition, the Prophet is related to have said that when Izrail approaches a believer he sits at his head and says "O pure soul, come forth to God's pardon and pleasure." And then the soul comes out as gently as water from a bag. But in the case of an infidel, the Angel of Death sits at his head and says, "O impure soul, come forth to the wrath of God!" And then the Angel of Death draws it out as a hot spit drawn out of wet wool (Mishkat Book V.Ch.III). Azrafel the third Principal Angel is in charge of the trumpet in the Last Days. The exact hour is not certain. However, the sure indication of the Day is when the blast of the trumpet is sounded by Azrafel. There will be three blasts, the blast of consternation, the blast of examination, and the blast of resurrection.

With the first blast, the earth will be shaken, mountains levelled, heavens melted, the sun darkened and the seas dried up. Confused and bewildered in the strange happenings, all creatures die, are struck with terror. When the blast of examination is blown, all creatures die, the last to die are the angels. Only God, Paradise and Hell and the Throne of Glory will exist. When the third and final blast is sounded, all the creatures are restored to life. The souls will fly forth like bees and fill the whole space between heaven and earth and rejoin their respective bodies. Thus the body and spirit are reunited for examination.

The fourth Archangel is Michael who cares for all created beings, that is to provide everything needed to them, and is a partner to Gabriel. The other angels in importance are Malik who presides over hell (Sura XLIII.7), Ridwan who guards Paradise and two angels known as Kiramun Katibun who record the good and evil deeds (Sura LXXX.15 and LXXXII, 10-12) of human beings. In view of the fact that the recording angel of evil stands on the left, the pious Muslims spit only on the left, and not on the right where stands the Angel of Good. There are also two angels Munkar and Nakir who examine the dead in the graves. Elaborate description of this are given in Traditional Literature. Eight angels of good rank are believed to be supporting the Throne of God, They are Hamalatul Arsh. Al-Baghawi, the famous Quran Commentator gives a graphic account of these angels. Standing from earth to heaven, they are so gigantic that it takes one to travel seven hundred years to cover the distance from ear to shoulder. Commentators have no unanimity regarding the place the angels occupy in Paradise. Probably, they occupy a lower province of the Paradise. The angels are next to the Faithful, the order being the Apostles, the Faithful and the Angels.

This also makes the Muslims to believe in Shayatin (Sing. Shaitan, Satan) made of fire and are supposed to be enemies of man. There are male and female shayatin. They can assume any shape and deceive human beings, but not the Apostles or Angels. Iblis was in fact an angel but was damned by God when he disobeyed His commands, to prostrate before Adam when all angels reverently obeyed. So the disobeyed Angel was driven out from Paradise and is called Iblis. Besides there are Jinns who were created from fire, but are grosser than angels. They also worship God. Unlike Shayatin, some of the Jinns are good. Others are bad. They eat and drink and are liable to death.

Al-Quran gives a vivid account of how jinns were obedient to Solomon the Prophet. An army of them worked for the family of David who employed them to build the Temple in Jerusalem. On Solomon's bidding, they worked for him day and night, making several big mansions and large dishes like fish ponds from each of which thousand men could eat at a time. And the rebel Jinns were severely whipped by the Angels for their disobedience by a whip of fire (Sura 34).

III. BELIEF IN THE REVEALED BOOKS

This is the third Belief of Islam. There are indications that one hundred and four Scriptures were delivered to mankind from time to time. Adam had received ten Scriptures, Seth fifty, Enoch thirty, Abraham ten, Moses, David, Jesus and Muhammad one each. Those received by Adam, Seth, Enoch and Abraham were inspired pamphlets (Sahifa) and the others were inspired Book (Kitab).[1] The former, so believe the devout Muslims, were lost to mankind, the latter are even now preserved but some of them not in its original purity. The inspired Books are Pentateuch (Taurat) of Moses (Sura LIII.37, LXXXVII.18) David's Psalms or Zabur (Sura IV.161 & XVII.57) the Gospel or Injil of Jesus (Sura V.50, 110 and LVII.27) and Al-Quran of Muhammad. The Islamic belief is that the first three Books lost much of their originality.

Al-Quran is a quintessence of all Scriptures and Islam is perfected with the preaching of Muhammad for in the Quran Allah says, "This day have I (Lord) perfected your Faith unto you, and fulfilled My mercy upon you, and appointed Islam for you to be your Religion."

Quran is to the very syllable "the word of God" (Kalam Allah) and the Book is called the "Book of Allah" (Kitab Allah). The Sacred Text is popularly known as 'Quran' meaning 'Recitation'. The book is also reputed to have fifty five other names.

Al - Kitab	=	The Book
Al - Mubin	=	The Enlightner
Al - Qra'n	=	The Reading
Al - Karim	=	The Good
Al - Kalam	=	The Word
Al - Burhan	=	The Proof
An - Nur	=	The Light
Al - Huda	=	The Guidance
Ar - Rahman	=	The Mercy
Al - Furqan	=	The Distinguisher

1. Jalaluddin As-Suyuti in his Itqan, p. 117.

Ash - Shifa	= The Health
Al - Mu'izah	= The Sermon
Az - Zikr	= The Reminder
Al - Mubarak	= The Blessed
Al - Ali	= The Lofty
Al - Hikmah	= The Wisdom
Al - Hakim	= The Philosopher
Al - Muhaimin	= The Preserver
Al - Musaddiq	= The Establisher of Truth
Al - Habl	= The Rope
As - Siratul Mustaqim	= The Straight Path
Al - Qaiyim	= The Strong
Al - Qaulu'l Fast	= The Distinguishing Speech
An - Naba'ul Azim	= The Exalted News
Al - Hasanu'l Hadis	= The Good Saying
Al - Masani	= The Repetition
Al - Mutashabih	= The Uniform
At - Tanzil	= The Revelation
Ar - Ruh	= The Spirit
Al - Wahy	= The Inspiration
Al - Arabi	= The Arabic
Al - Basair	= The Enlightenment
Al - Bayan	= The Explanation
Al - 'Ilm	= The Knowledge
Al - Haqq	= The Truth
Al - Hadi	= The Guide
Al - Ajab	= The Wonderful
At - Tazkirah	= The Exhortation
Al - Urwatu'l Wasqa	= The Firm Handle
As - Sidq	= The Righteous
Al - 'Adl	= The Justice
Al - Amr	= The Order
Al - Munadi	= The Preacher
Al - Bushra	= The Glad Tidings
Al - Majid	= The Exalted
Az - Zabur	= The Psalm
Al - Bashir	= The Herald of Glad Tidings
An - Nazir	= The Warner
Al - Aziz	= The Mighty
Al - Balagh	= The Message

Al - Qasas	=	The Narrative
As - Suhuf	=	The Pamphlets
Al - Mukarramah	=	The Excellent
Al - Marfwah	=	The Exalted
Al - Mutaharah	=	The Purified

The Arabic route of the word Quran is from Qara, the first verse revealed to the Prophet (Sura XCV) meaning 'to recite'. Hence Quran means 'A Recitation' especially meant to recite during religious functions. It is also called Al-Quran al-Majid (The Glorious Quran), Al-Quran Ash-Sharif (the Noble Quran) and Furqan (Distinguisher). Or, simply Al-Kitab (the Book).

The Traditionalists believe that Al-Quran is 'uncreated' and is eternal and it existed in the heaven (Sura XLIII.3, XIII,39, III.5) in a form written by God before it was lowered to the lowest heaven. They say that the Quran was written on the Preserved Tablet (Al-Lawh-Al-Mahfuz) (Sura LXXXV. 22) and it was brought down and kept in Baitul Izza (Mighty House) in the lowest heaven nearest to earth on the Night of Decree (Laylatul Qadr). Some say, the entire Quran was lowered all at once while others say, part by part, to the extent of verses for one year's revelation was brought down at one time. It is from Baitul Izza that Gabriel (Sura II.91) brought it to the Prophet verse after verse, revealing the entire book in twenty-two years or a little more of his prophetic career. It is probable that Gaberial brought down to the Prophet only the meaning of Al-Quran and the proper wording to these meanings might have been given by the Prophet himself.[1]

If the whole Text is uncreated, doubted some, what about the statements and reports purported to have been said by the Prophets, human beings and even by satan which are quoted at random in the Sacred Text. To this, the Traditionalists found an answer. Quran undoubtedly is God's uncreated word, but the words of Moses, Pharaoh and Satan are created so far they are concerned. However the reports as reproduced in the Quran are the words of God and so uncreated.

At the time of the Prophet's death, there were 1,44,000 Sahaba (Companions) who had actually lived with the Prophet at least for some

---

[1] It is disputed by many. Some say that the clothing of expression was done by Gabriel himself and then revealed to the Prophet.

time. Many of them were experts in the knowledge of the Quran. Until the death of the Prophet, there was no necessity to codify it. However, after the battle of Yamama just one year after the Prophet's death, an unusual situation arose when many of the Quran reciters were killed. Accordingly, the first copy of Quran was compiled by Zaid, one of the principal amanuensis of the Prophet. Within fifteen years during the rule of Uthman, the third Caliph a revision was necessitated for Quran differing from the authentic copy existed in different parts of Arabia. Again, Zaid made a scrutiny of all these unauthorised versions and made an authentic one. When it was ready, all the unauthorised copies were destroyed. It is truly astonishing that Quran retained its original purity during all these centuries. Ever since that day, not a word is changed. It is read and re-read by millions of people all over the Islamic world with solemn piety and devotion.

> *"This Book (Al-Quran) is a veritable proof from your Lord, a guide and a blessing to true believers."*
> *"When the Quran is recited, listen to it in silence so that Allah may show you mercy. Remember your Lord deep in your soul with humility and reverence, and without ostentation: remember Him morning and evening, and do not be neglected." (Sura VII. The Heights/Al-Araf.)*

All the Suras begin with the ejaculation "Bismillah" except Sura IX probably because it appears as a continuation of the previous sura. It is translated as, "In the Name of Allah, the Compassionate, the Merciful" or "In the Name of Merciful and Compassionate". The ejaculation "Bismillah" is very important in the life of a Muslim. He utters it before all ceremonies, before he eats, bathes, when he undertakes a journey. He says it whenever an animal is slaughtered otherwise the meat is unlawful to eat.

Quran is revealed in Arabic and recorded in Arabic. And the Arabic of the Quran is by turns "striking, soaring, vivid, terrible, tends and breathtaking."[1] Its "flashing images and inexorable measures go directly to the brain and intoxicate it."[2]

Fatiha or the Opening Sura also called the Chapter of Thanksgiving is the essence of Quran and is recited in every worship and on every important occasion. In reality, it is a prayer, exordium. It is held

---

[1] & [2] Dr. J.A. Williams, *Islam*. p. 16 Prentice-Hall International, London

in high esteem that hardly a function both public and private passes without recitation of Fatiha[1]. Its importance is stressed in Al-Quran. In Sura Al Hejr XV, it is said: "We have given you the seven repeated verses and the Glorious Koran.'' Sura Ya Sin XXXVI, is called the Qulbul Quran (the heart of the Quran)[2]. Many of the Quranic verses have special importance. Reciting the Ayatul Fath or the Verse of Victory (59th verse of Suratul Anam-VI) constantly will fulfil one's desire. And ayatul Hifz or the Verse of Protection (Sura II.256, Sura XII.64, Sura XIII.12, Sura XV.17 and Sura XXXVII.7) are considered protective in nature and many divotees write them in amulets for wearing on their persons to escape from evil spirits and evil eyes. If a person repeats Ayatul Kursi[3] or the Verse of Throne (Sura II.256) after each worship, nothing prevents him from entering Paradise. The twelfth verse of Sura (Ayatul Mawaris)-IV is the foundation of Islamic Law. Similarly, there are verses denoting Allah's names and His qualities and they are par excellence. Ayatul Kursi has a charm of its own. The following is Pickthall's English rendering of it:

"Allah! There is no God save Him, the Alive, the Eternal. Neither slumber nor sleep overtaketh Him. Unto Him belongeth whatsoever is in the heavens and whatsoever is in the earth. Who is he that intercedeth with Him save by His leave? He knoweth that which is in front of them and that which is behind them, while they encompass nothing of His knowledge saw what He will. His throne includeth the heavens and the earth, and He is never weary of preserving them. He is the sublime, the Tremendous." (Sura II. 255)

Meccan and Medinan Suras

The verses received by the Prophet prior the Hijrat constitute the

---

[1] In the name of Allah, the Compassionate, the Merciful.
Praise be to Allah, Lord of the Creation
The Compassionate, the Merciful
King of Judgment-day
You alone we worship, and to You alone we pray for help
Guide us to the straight path
The path of those whom You have favoured,
Not of those who have incurred Your wrath,
Nor of those who have gone astray." (Amen)

[2] Prophet Muhammad when his house was besieged by the rebels, escaped in the dead of night by reciting the first nine verses of Ya Sin, unnoticed by the guards who were seized with a coma, slept for a while until the God's Messenger was safe.

[3] The name of Throne is Corsi which is the tribunal or seat of justice. It is the divine providence.

Meccan Suras. In fact, it includes all pre-Hijra Suras whether the Prophet received the revelation in Mecca or elsewhere. While the Medinan Suras are post-Hijrat. In contents, they differ very much for Meccan Suras have plenty of striking imagery. They deal with the reality of a future life, of Paradise and hell, of the Last Day, resurrection and the Judgement. On the contrary, Medinan suras are prosaic. They mostly deal with the state and its working, about the various battles fought in the early days of Islam etc. The Book as a whole is so sacred that no grown up Muslim dare to touch it without first taking the ablution.

The complete Book consists of some 6239[1] verses (Ayat) arranged in 114 Suras (not exactly chapters). Literally Sura means a row, an order or anything in series. Some of the suras are short: the smallest sura only three verses and the longest (Sura entitled Cow) has 286 verses. The arrangement of the suras appears to have no chronological sequence, the longest suras appear in the last next to the Opening Sura (Al-Fatiha) and short ones in the beginning. Every sura has a title; most of these titles have a bearing with the text of the sura. Some of these titles have a mystery of their own for they remain unexplained. There are in all 29 suras beginning with similar titles. For example. A.L.M. of Sura 2. Some commentators say "A" stands for Allah,"L" for Latif (Gracious) and "M" for Majid (Glorious). Another opinion is that it meant for Ana' Llahu A'lamu (I am the God who knoweth). Some others say that it is a mystery not meant to understand. Similarly, the title 'Ya Sin' (Sura XXXVI) is unexplained. Al Baizawi says that it means Ya Saiyd (O Saiyid); Jalan says that God only knows its meaning.

The Quran is absolute. Its words, whether secular or spiritual are faithfully followed by the people of the Prophet. As seen earlier, it prescribes its votaries certain acts to perform such as prayer, alms-tax, fasting etc. It has also negative precepts, such as prohibition of wine, Games of chance, accepting of usury, eating swine's flesh and carrion etc. Perhaps no piece of legislation has ever succeeded to the extent of Quran.

---

[1] Kufah version followed in Kufa and India. Besides there are four versions-Shami (6225 verses) followed in Syria, Makkah (6219 verses) followed in Mecca, Medinah (6211 verses) followed in Medinah, and Basrah (6204 verses) followed in Busrah. The Quran contains 77,639 words or 323,015 letters.

in eliminating many of the social evils. Drinking wine, lending money for usury and games of chance are taboo in the Islamic world and most of the Muslims follow these precepts so faithfully that they lead a perfect life. They are good people. Quran reprimands its followers from entering a house without permission. "Greet each other, seek the permission and then enter" is the golden rule prescribed for the votaries of Islam to enter a house. Making others know your presence is so important an act that it is known as Istizan (Sura XXIV.27-29). Similarly, there is the Quranic injunction how to greet a person (Sura XXIV. 61) and how to return a greeting (Sura IV. 88). Combined with these Quranic injunctions are scores of Prophet's practices which together form a perfect system of man's conduct towards God and towards fellow beings. Quranic prescription containing laws governing man's conduct towards God is called Ibadat and that governing human relations is called Mu'malat. The entire Islamic world consider Al-Quran as a miracle—as the only miracle the Prophet Muhammad (PBUH) had as a proof of his apostleship. To show its superiority, the enemies of Islam were challenged to compose one chapter similar to Quran and despite their best efforts, they could not bring forth a sentence equivalent to any of the Quranic verses. This speaks of its greatness.

Quran is for the entire mankind. It undoubtedly recognises all the Prophets. It says; We sent before you other apostles to their people. (Sura The Greeks 30) This theme is repeated in several passages. The reader who likes to know them may read Sura 2, 10, 11, 12, 19, 26, 27, 28, 29, 34, 37, 40, 42, 43, 51, 54, 57, 59, 61, 68, 69, and 79.

Al- Quran is the essence of all the scriptures; a sum total of wisdom and knowledge of all previous revelations. Its basic teaching is to bring the mankind to submit to the Lord of creation for which it prescribes certain duties. Five of them are most important whose faithful performance makes a man what he is and what he ought to be. Those who keep away from them aro sinners; severe punishment is waiting upon them. Quran gives a graphic account of punishment for the wrong and eternal bliss for the righteous. Provided for the Servants of Allah are mansions and "by their side sit bashful dark-eyed, as chaste as the sheltered eggs of Ostrich. "(Sura The Ranks 3). "Reclining upon soft couches they will gaze around them; and in their faces you shall make the glow of joy. They shall drink of a pure wine, securely sealed, whose very dregs are musk (for this let all men emulously strive); a wine tempered with the waters of Tasnim, a spring at which the favoured will refresh themselves." (The Unjust. Sura 83)[1] Who then are the righteous? "The true servants of the Merciful are those who walk humbly on the earth and say: 'Peace!' to the ignorant who accost them; who pass the night standing and on their knees in adoration of their Lord; who say: 'Lord, ward off from us the punishment of Hell, for its punishment is everlasting: an evil dwelling and an evil resting place,' who are neither extravagant nor niggardly but keep the golden mean, who invoke no other god besides Allah and do not kill except for a just cause, (manslaughter is forbidden by Him), who do not commit adultery (he that does this shall meet with evil. His punishment shall be doubled on the Day of Resurrection and in disgrace he shall abide for ever—unless he repent and believe and do good works, for then Allah will change his sins to good actions. Allah is forgiving and merciful. He that repents and does good work truly returns to Allah), who do not bear false witness and do not lose their dignity when listening to profane abuse, who do not turn a blind eye and a deaf ear to the revelations of their Lord when they are reminded of them, who say. 'Lord, give us joy in our wives and children and make us examples to those who fear you.' These shall be rewarded with Paradise for their fortitude. There, they shall find a welcome and a greeting, and there they shall abide for ever, a blessed dwelling and a blessed resting place." (Al-Furqan, Sura 25)

On the Resurrection Day, all the evil doers shall collect to receive the reward of their misdeeds. A voice will cry: Cast into Hell every hardened unbeliever, every opponent of good works, and every doubting transgressor who has set up another god besides Allah. Hurl them into the fierce, tormenting flames." (Qaf. Sura 50). And ever hungry Hell will ask for more and more sinners. There, in the Hell, all the wicked, the sinners and the Disbelievers will recieve a stern punishment. The hell fire would scorch their faces and they would writhe in pain. To add to their misery, scalding water as hot as molten brass would be given to them for drinking and fruits of Zaqqum-tree which sprouts out from the interior of hell having fruits like devil's head for food.

The teachings of Al-Quran are sincere, frank, direct and appealing. The warning contained in Sura 80, "He Frowned" which refers a minor event in the Life of the Prophet who rebuked a blind man who had come to the Prophet for guidance, is an all time lesson for the Muslims.

---

[1] Read also Sura 78 (The Tidings), Sura 69 (The Inevitable)

Quran also gives a vivid description about the creation and the Day of Judgement. "Allah has created the heavens in six days and then ascended His throne, ordaining all things." Then He has created man from potter's clay and the Jinn from smokeless fire. (The Merciful. Sura 55). He has given the bounties of the earth for the full enjoyment of human beings but with a warning not to go astray and become atheist or idolaters. Each man is attended by two keepers, one sitting on his left and the other, on his right recording everything spoken and done by him. Not an atom's weight in earth or heaven escapes God's knowledge, not there is any object smaller or greater but is not recorded. On the Judgement Day, this Book will be produced. No soul shall bear another's burden and that each man shall be judged by his own labours. "On that day the Trumpet shall be sounded and you shall come in multitudes. The gates of heaven shall swing open and the mountains shall pass away and become like vapour." (The Tidings. Sura 78) The righteous get the book in their right hands and the condemned would receive it in their left hands. And for the Servants of Allah, Paradise will be brought close to them God will say: "Enter in peace. This is the day of immortality. There they will have all that they desire."

The melody of the Quran is superb, especially when it is heard wafting through the still night. Its music dives deep into the heart. The real achievement of the Quran is its telling manifold ideas in each Sura so that the readers are not tired of reading the same theme over and over again. The Quranic words are selective and apt giving a true picture of what they meant. They are forceful and authoritative when ownership is concerned, as in "We are the Heir of all things;" frightening when the Day of Judgement and Torments of Hell are described; tempting and even sensual when the Bliss of Paradise is told. Harsh to Unbelievers, Sinners, thieves and wicked, Kind to Orphans and slaves, Quran promises rich reward for all good works. It forewarns that "actions as small as a grain of mustard seed shall be weighed out." (The Prophet, Sura 21) Another astonishing fact about Al-Quran is its simplicity. Its allegories, allusions and similies are everyday talks[1] that even an

---

[1]However the writer has to confess regretfully that he could not understand only one Quanic Passage despite his many readings.

"Allah is the light of the heavens and the earth. His light may be compared to a niche that enshrines a lamp, the lamp within a crystal of star-like brilliance. It is lit from a blessed olive tree neither eastern nor western. Its very oil would almost shine forth, though no fire touched it, Light upon light, Allah guides to His light whom He will" (Light, Sura 24). Its meanings one perhaps fatheomless and deep for us to reach.

illiterate desert wanderer can easily grasp it as in "Barren soil yields poor fruit". Every desert dweller knows what grows below his feet. Again, the works of Unbelievers are compared to mirages which fool the thirsty travellers. No Arab need to be told what mirage is! At the same time, it is a great warning to those weary travellers who are in pursuit of knowledge not to be fooled by the mirages. "On that day we shall roll up the heaven like a scroll of parchment." (The Prophet, Sura 21). By this single sentence, God's Authority, His Power and Strength is well established. Now let us see, how God's omnipresence is expressed in Quran. "If three men talk in secret together, He is their fourth, if four, He is their fifth, if five, He is their sixth, whether fewer or more wherever they be He is with them." (She who Pleaded, Sura 58).

The early Arabs who were passionate lovers of poetry were intoxicated in its sublime beauty. It is narrated that Prophet Muhammad used to recite it in an appealing voice, often emphasising the words so that his listeners become attentive. Whenever he was reciting the verses depicting the torments of hell, his voices went up and low, often raising his fingers for emphasis. His immediate successor, Hadhrat Abu Bakr could seldom read the Quran without shedding tears. There are now many who could recite it in the same strain, as the stalwarts of Islam could do it, not long ago.

The healing powers of Quranic verses are unsurpassable, believes the orthodox, and in sickness, many of the passages are read to the patients. Verses of the Throne (Ayatul Khursi) excell all others and its recitation has special merit. Devout Muslims recite it as often as possible. Some others write it in amulets and carry it on their person. Muslim physicians (Hakim) write it in plates with black ink obtained from burnt rice and make a potion of it with water to be given as a sure panacea for insomnia, fear etc. Surprisingly, many find solace in it. It is said that the Prophet left Mecca on a crucial night unnoticed by the guards who had cast a net of themselves around his home to kill him, by reciting the first few verses of Surah Yasin.[1] Suddenly they were seized in a coma, insensitive to the surroundings, and Lo! the Prophet had fled through the very eyes of his enemies. They shook themselves out of the seizure when the Prophet was safe in the darkness.

When this book was being written, a devotee had confessed to me that he had won the love of his enemy by a short course of reciting constantly Sura Yasin. The modus operandi of this unusual devotional

---

[1]Sura Yasin is considered as the Heart of Quran reciting it is highly meritorius.

exercise is like this: Arising from his sleep at 2 a.m. every day, he used to have his normal ablutions, and read Surah Yasin from beginning until the first occurrence of the word 'Mubeen' (verse) and then re-read it from the beginning until he read the second 'Mubeen' (verse). Again he turned back to the beginning and read the text until the third 'Mubeen' (verse). This was repeated eight times as there are seven Mubeen in Surah Yasin. This was followed by a special prayer and Du'a. He continued this excersise for forty days and at the end, he had indication that he had won the war without firing a single shot. His former enemy is now his best friend.

No Muslim ever touches the Quran without legal ablution. It is always kept on the top. Reading it on any day is meritorious; however reading it on auspicious days like Friday, Monday and Thursday has special rewards. With moderate speed, one can read a Juz a day covering the whole book in 30 days. On rapid reading, many complete it in a week.[1]

Many are the Quranic verses often quoted:
"Evil shall recoil on those that plot evil." (Sura 35 The Creator).
"Truth has come. Falsehood has vanished and shall return no more." (Sura 34 Sheba)
"To your Lord you shall all return." (Sura 32 Adoration)
"God is close to him than the veins of his neck."
Requit evil with good."
"No soul shall bear another's burden and each man shall be judged by his own labours." (Sura 56 Star)
"Finest of all garment is the robe of piety." (Sura 7 The Heights)

IV. BELIEF IN THE APOSTLE

The fourth article of Dogma is belief in the apostles. Quranic teaching is that "for every nation there is a messenger." (Sura X. 48). Again it is given in Sura XXXV. 24: "And there is not a nation but a warner hath passed among them". God pardoned Adam despite his disobeyal and bestowed on him the Divine Light which was transmitted from him

---

[1]To facilitate easy reading, identification marks are made in Quran. i.e., its 77,934 words (114 Suras) are set in 10 Ruku or Sections. Rub is quarter of Juz, Nisf, half of Juz, Sul, three quarter of Juz and Manzil mark the 7 stages (dividing the Quran into 7 divisions enabling one to read each division in one day).

to Noah, Abraham etc until it was finalised and perfected in Muhammad. Thus Islam according to its Sacred Text was the religion of Adam, Noah, Abraham, Moses and Jesus and to all the apostles, and obviously any one who does not believe in the heaven-sent apostles departs from the dogma of Islam. That means he becomes a disbeliever. We have just seen that Muslims also believe in Jesus but their belief slightly varies from that of Christians. They believe him not as the son of God and that he was born in a miraculous manner,[1] and probably he died a natural death. His end is variously given. There are many who believe that he had escaped to India. In Japan, they believe that Jesus took asylum in their country and lived a long life.

Al-Quran mentions about two types of inspired men—Nabi and Rusul. Nabi (Plural Anbiya) is one who has received direct inspiration (Wahy) by means of an angel or by inspiration of the heart. In short, Nabi is any one directly inspired by God who preaches and gives warnings. Rasul (Plural Rusul) is a Messenger who has recieved a book through an angel. Quran also uses the word Mursal (Plural Mursalun) for Messenger. So all Rusul are Anbiya, and not all Anbiya, Rusul.

Tradition records about 1000 to 222,000 Prophets and 315 apostles.[2] Some 28 names of Apostles occur in the Quran: Adam, Idris (Enoch), Noah, Hud (Heber), Salih (Methusaleh), Abraham, Ismael, Isaac, Yaqub (Jacob), Yusuf (Joseph), Lut (Lot), Musa (Moses), Harun (Aaron), Shu'aib (Jethro), Zackariya, Yahya (John), Isa (Jesus), David, Sulaiman (Solomon), Ilyas (Elias), Alyasa (Elisha), Aiyub (Job), Yunus (Jonah), Uzair (Ezra), Luqman (Aesop), Zu'l-Kife (Isaiah or Abadiah,) Zul-Qurnain[1] and Muhammad.

Besides there are three women Prophetess, Sarah, Mother of Moses, and Mary the daughter of Imran, for Sarah received by revelation the news of Isac's birth, the birth of Moses was divinely commanded to his mother, and Mary received the glad tidings of the birth of Jesus from angel.

Allah prefers some of the messengers, excel others (Sura II. 253 and Sura XVII. 55). Nine apostles are called Ulul Azm as they possess

---

[1] Because of this belief of Muslims, they are a sort of heterodox Christians. The Muslims belief of Jesus as an Apostle and in the Divine Book (Gospel), they deny him as the Son of God, or do not equate him with God. God has no consort.

[2]Mishkat Book XXIV. Ch. 1 p. 3 gives only 1,24,000 Prophets and 315 Apostles. Ibn Sa'd says 1,000. Reland says 2,24,000.

[1]It is not clearly established whether Zul Qarnain is Alexander the Great or not.

constancy. They are Noah, Abraham, David, Jacob, Joseph, Job, Moses, Jesus and Muhammad. Six apostles are known to have special titles. Adam (Safi'llah, the chosen of God), Noah (Nabiyu'llah, The Preacher of God), Abraham (Khalilu llah, the Friend of God), Moses (Kalimu llah, the Converser with God), Jesus (Ruhu llah, the Spirit of God), and Muhammad (Rasulu llah, the Messenger of God). Probably others are minor Prophets.

Muhammad is God's Messenger (Resul Allah) for the Islamic Creed says "Muhammad Rasul Allah." That is he is a Messenger, pure and simple. On the contrary Nabi is a preacher, a Prophet. Islam was the religion of all the heaven-sent apostles. In the Quran, Sura III. verse 19 it is said that the religion with Allah is Islam. Previously five Prophets had preached in Arabic, namely Hud, Saleh, Abraham, Ismael and Shoaib. But Muhammad is the Rasul through whom God has perfected the imperfect preachings of the earlier Prophets. That is, Muhammad is the Seal of the Prophets. (Quran Sura XXXIII. 40). In other words every Muslim believes Muhammad as the climax of man's evolution. Belief in the final Prophethood of Muhammad is so important an article of Faith, that the Prophet said, "he who has seen me has seen God." There is a passage in the Quran stating that Muhammad is the Messenger not for a nation or for some people as the earlier Prophets heve been, but he is "a Warner unto all mankind." (Sura XXXIV. 28)

Muhammad was manifestation of truth, of beauty and of strength. He was so virtuous and noble that one day Hadhrat Ali had said of him: "Whoever see him will not feel his thirst or hunger". Muhammad was so faithfully devoted to the special mission entrusted to him by God that he got little time, very little time indeed to be swayed by in the beauties of this world. He often reminded his companions that in this world we are like travellers only. We stay for a little time and pass on. Above all God's Messenger was simple and frugal. His simplicity was shocking to his own companions. They simply imitated the 'Master' and all of them were equally simple, but certainly not as simple as the Messenger. From his death bed, he called for the only five dinars he got in his house to be given in charity. Within hours, he died lying in the hands of his favourite wife, Aisha. This faith in his own mission, this sincercity, this love to fellow beings, this simplicity, this strenght and above all this unflinching loyalty to God made him as the greatest apostle ever preached in this world.

Muhammad was a fine blend of Muhammad as a man, as the only

son of Abdullah (Muhammad ibn Abdullah), and Muhammad as the Messenger of God (Rasul Allah). As a man, Muhammad was superb, but as the Messenger of God he had excelled all. With a touch of optimism in his outlook that moved mountains, he worked hard day and night, often starving and at risk of his own life until he succeeded in delivering the true religion of God of its dross of polytheism and idolatry. He never performed miracles. On the contrary he vehemently denied that he was a performer of miracles. He lived as any other man struggling to earn his livelihood, but in complete submission to the Will of God. He used to pray often but never overdid it. He observed fast and used to break it at the appointed times; he performed Pilgrimage accompanied by his followers on the appointed days. Without claiming any superiority from others, he suffered the strains of the journey under the inhospitable desert sun across the desert. Like any other man he had married and had children. He said that marriage is half religion. Another prophetic saying is, "a virtuous wife is a man's best treasure."The essential virtues that distinguished a Prophet from other creation were excelled in Muhammad for God made easy things hard to him and difficulties were lightened to him. Foremost of the easy things made difficult to him were that, as the Apostle of God, he had to observe supererogatory worships even during midnight and that he was forbidden to accept anything given in charity. It is reported that one day he made his grandchildren, Imam Hasan and Imam Husain to omit a few dates eaten by them, as the fruits were given in charity. He was also forbidden to remove cloak of arms before the enemy was met. The story was that during the Battle of Uhud, a decision was taken to meet the enemies who were camping in the plains of Uhud. Accordingly after the noon prayer was said, the Apostles retired to his chamber and re-appeared in uniform to lead his followers to Uhud. Suddenly some of his followers resented the earlier decision as hasty and wrong. Thereupon, the Prophet said that it was unbecoming of a prophet to remove the uniform until the enemy was met. The other virtues of a Prophet were that he was prevented from casting any surreptious and passionate look, and from writing poetry etc. It was also forbidden for him to eat while reclining and strong smelling vegetables such as garlic, onion, leek etc.

One of the difficult things lightened to him was the number of wives he could have such as a Prophet. He was permitted to marry more than four wives; he could also marry in the pilgrimage garb, if he would so desire. The Prophet was also not forbidden to shed blood 'even within the sacred territory and was permitted to observe fast lasting two days and two nights. His sleeping would not invalidate Wudu or ceremonial ablution. Prophet could enter a mosque even if he was in Jaban (defiled). He was also permitted to judge a case on the basis of his own reason.

V. BELIEF IN THE LAST DAY AND THE RESURRECTION

This belief is based on the immortality of soul and the reality of a future life. There is a last Day; and Resurrection or Al-Yaumul Akhir or Yaumul Qiyam is a certainty. References about this belief are plenty in Al-Quran. They occur in Sura II.79, Sura LXXVII-14, Sura XL.28, Sura XXX.56, Sura I.3, Sura XI.85, Sura VII 186, Sura LXXV.3, Sura XI.83, Sura VII.186, Sura LXXV, Sura LXXXI. 1-19, Sura LXXXII. Sura LXXXIII 4-20, Sura LXXXIV. 1-19 and in Sura XXII. 1-7) The approach of the Last Day will be preceded by certain signs-8 Lesser signs (Isharatu-Sa'ah) and 17 Greater Signs (Alamatus Sa'ah)

The Lesser Signs

1. The decay of faith among men.
2. Mean and worthless persons rising to eminence
3. Men will lose interest in religious matters, and they will be more interested in sexsual pleasures so that maid servants bear children of their masters.
4. Tumults and seditions.
5. There will be an outbreak of war probably with the Greeks or with the Romans
6. The world will have more distress and calamity. Wickedness and violence will prevail.
7. The provinces of al-Iraq and Syria stop paying tribute.
8. The buildings of al-Medina shall reach to as far as Mecca.

The Greater Signs

1. The sun will rise in the west.
2. A monster called Dabbatul Arz having the head of a bull, the ears of an elephant, the horns of a stag, the neck of an ostrich, the breast of a lion, the colour of a tiger, the back of a cat, the

tail of a ram, the leg of a camel, and the voice of an ass will appear thrice in several places. Its swift movement makes overtaking it imposible.

3. In a war with the Romans or Greeks, Constantinople will fall to some 70,000 descendants of Isaac.
4. The coming of Anti-Christ (Dajjal) an one-eyed false or lying Christ bearing on his brow the letters "KFR" signifying unbelief who will ride a white ass for 40 days (equal to 440 ordinary days. One day is equal to one year, another to a month, another to a week and the rest will be ordinary days. Totalling all these will be equal to 440 days). He will ride on until he is slain by Jesus.
5. The descent of Jesus on earth, near the white tower to the east of Damascus and conduct the mid-day prayer. Then he will slay the Anti-Christ at the gates of Lyda. He will marry and have children. He will rule the world for 40 years.
6. Wars with the Jews.
7. The re-appearance of the barbarous tribes Gog and Magog and in the end they will be destroyed.
8. Clouds of smoke will fill the earth.
9. Three eclipses of the moon, one in the east, another in the west and the third in Arabia will be seen.
10. Al-Lat and Al-Uzza will be worshipped especially in Arabia.
11. The river Euphrates will retreat, revealing heaps of gold and silver. This exposed wealth will be the cause of destruction of many.
12. Demolition of Ka'ba by Ethiopians.
13. Speaking of inanimate things.
14. An out break of fire in the province of al-Hijaz.
15. A descendant of Kahtan will drive men before him with his staff.
16. The coming of Mahdi, that is one from the family of the Prophet.
17. A wind shall blow and sweep away the souls of all who have but a grain of faith in their hearts.

In the Hadith literature, there is a Saying of Prophet related by Anas. He says that "the Prophet had said. 'Verily decay of wisdom, ignorant people, drinking and open adultery are signs of the approach of Last Day'." (Imam Bukhari)

This naturally leads us to a question regarding the intermediate period—the period after the death and the Last Day. Citing the following story, the orthodox Muslims say that there is punishment in the Tomb. It is narrated by Zaid ibn Thabit that one day when some of the Companions were with the Apostle, his mule, usually calm and quiet, agitated as if frightened by the ghastly appearance of some six graves belonging to the Banu Al-Najjar. The Apostle immediately asked, "When did these people (buried there) die?" Zaid said, "In the time of polytheism". Thereupon, he said." Verily they are tormented in their graves________" Turning to them, he said twice. "Take refuge with Allah from the punishment in the grave." Al-Quran also gives not elob-oratly punishment in the graves. For example in Sura LX.101, it is given, "We know them, and we shall chastice them twice; they will be relegated to a painful doom."[1] Commentators differ in many details about the interrogation of the soul in the Tomb. Some say the punishment will last on the approach of the next Friday. Another opinion is that it will continue till the Last Day, suspending it on Fridays and Ramadan months. Whatever be the duration of the punishment in the Tomb, the common belief is that two black angels with blue eyes, Munkar and Nakir will cause the dead man to sit up in the grave asking, "Who is thy Lord, and what is thy religion, and who is thy Prophet?" Even if there is no questioning in the graves, the dead remain in their Tombs until the Day of Judgement. It is likely that the souls of the Apostle would enter the Paradise directly without any waiting. However, some other belief is that they would be admitted to some intermediate place called Araf. Regarding the souls of the created beings, we can presume from the narration of the Prophet or his NIGHT JOURNEY that they will reach the lowest heaver. These destined for Paradise occupy the heaven on the right of Adam and the condemned souls reach the left hand side. Some others are inclined to believe that the souls will find a place inside the trumpet and stay there until the Last Day.

The Djahmites,[2] firm believers in the Absolute Unity of God (Tawhid) however say that beside God nothing is Eternal. Even Quran, Paradise and Hell are created and are not Eternal because God is the Absolute, the Only Creator, the only Eternal Being. There is no second Eternal. Hence they disbelieve the concept of Reward and Punishment either in the grave, or Paradise and Hell.

---

[1]Other verse mentioning punishment of the grave is in Sura LII.47 "And verily, for those who do wrong, there is a punishment beyond that." It is the common belief that the animals could hear mysterious noises originating from the graves; could feel the strange sense of foreboding when they approach graves. Supporting this, orthodox even cite the following story. The Prophet's beast had a shiver and shrieked on approaching a grave. Prophet confirmed that animals could perceive punishment in the graves.

[2]The followers of Djalm ibn Saffwan.

The exact hour of resurrection also is uncertain. However, it begins with the first blast of the trumpet or the blast of consternation. It will be blown by Israfil and will be so terrific that all creatures struck with terror will run helter-skelter. The earth will shake in its firmaments, the mountains will be levelled, the sun loses its brightness and the seas begin to dry up. The following is a graphic account of this day as given in the Sacred Text.

"The day when the sky will become as molten copper
and the hills become as flakes of wool,
and no familiar friend will ask a question of his friend,
Though they will be given sight of them. The guilty man will long be able to ransome himself from the punishment of that day at the price of his children
And his spouce and his brother
And his kin that harboured him
And all that are in the earth, if then it might deliver him
But nay! for lo! it is the fire of hell
Eager to roast;
It calleth him who turned and fled (from truth),
And hoarded (wealth) and withheld it." (Sura LXX. 8-18)
Again
"A day wherein manking will be as thickly-scattered moths
And the mountains will become as carded wool. (Sura 101. verse 4 & 5)
When the sun is overthrown,
And when the starts fall
And when the hills are moved
And when the camels big with young are abandoned,
And when the wild beasts are herded together,
And when the seas rise,
And when the souls are reunited,
And when the girl-child that was buried alive is asked
For what sin she was slain,
And when the pages are laid open,
And when the sky is torn away,
And when hell is lighted,
And when the garden is brought night,

It is followed by the second blast or Blast of Examination (Nafkh Al-Bath). In swift movements, all creatures will die except God, Paradise and Hell, and the Throne of Glory. This is followed by a rain for forty years. At the end of the fortieth year, the third blast known as the blast of Resurrection will be blown. With the sounding of the third blast, all souls will be gathered along with the bodies in perfect condition. Then begins the Judgement lasting for thousand years (Sura XXXII.4) or fifty thousand years. (Sura LXX.4). It is probable that for Judgement all the creatures will assemble in a plain (probably in the earth) and it takes years together (Commentators differ. Some say it takes forty years only. Others seventy, thirty, fifty thousand years) before the Judgement proper takes place. During this interval, the 'just' suffer less on account of their good deeds while the wicked suffer heavily. Their faces become blackened and disfigured. It is also believed that the sun will shine just above their heads only a mile up that the skulls of the wicked will boil; the sweat flows down forming pools. In the end, God will appear in the clouds. God will come with angels, rank on rank. (Sura 89. verse 22). Every creature is examined with the help of the Book of Record of all the words and deeds. All actions will be weighed on the scales of Mizan (Balance)[1]. (Comments of the Quranic passage differ. Some say the Book will be weighed, others say only words and actions will be weighed). However, every person is judged on the basis of his good and bad works.

Then the just and the unjust pass through a bridge (As-sirat)[2] stretched over the back of hell. It is thinner than a hair and sharper than the edge of a sword. The first to pass through the bridge will be the Prophet who will simply walk over the bridge uttering "Allahumma Sallim, Sallim." However, the just will pass with the swiftness of lightning, and the wicked and the unjust stumble over it and fall headlong into the hell below. The righteous, both men and women thus enter the Paradise. "Lo ! men who surrender unto Allah, and women who

---

[1]Mawazin Plural. The scales are so vast in size that they can hold both heaven and earth. The Balance will be held by Gabriel. The scales hang over Paradise and Hell. The Quranic passage is simple, as follows:

"Then, as for him whose scales are heavy (with good works)
He will live a pleasant life"
But as for him whose scales are light,
The Bereft and Hungry One will be his mother,
Ah, what will convey unto thee what she is!
Raging fire." (Sura 101, verse 6-11)

[2]This is chiefly based on the interpretation of the Traditionalists. Some Commentators interpret the fire in verse 71 of Sura XIX as bridge.

surrender, and men who believe and women who believe, and men who obey and women who obey, and men who speak the truth, and women who speak the truth, and men who preserve (in righteousness) and women whom preserve, and men who are humble and women who are humble, and men who give alms and women who give alms, and men who fast and women who fast, and men who guard their modesty and women who guard (their modesty) and men who remember—Allah hath prepared for them forgiveness and a vast reward." (Sura 33, verse 35)

Quran accepts seven heavens (Sura 41. verse 12 & Sura 78. verse 12) and also many gardens are mentioned. In Sura 55 (verses 46 & 62) is mentioned four such gardens. However, Quran Commentators mention eight such gardens in Paradise (Al-Jannah). They are:

1. Jannatul Khuld (Garden of Eternity)
2. Darus Salam (Dwelling of Peace)
3. Darul Qarar (Dwelling which abideth)
4. Jannatul Adn (Garden of Eden)
5. Jannatul Ma'wa (Garden of Refuge)
6. Jannatul Naim (Garden of Delight)
7. Illiyun, and
8. Jannatul Firdaus (Garden of Paradise)

The prospective entrants to Paradise quench their thirst from the pond of the Prophet (Haud). There are beautiful tents in Paradise to live in. Exquisite foods and delicious fruits will be provided for the Blessed in Paradise. (Sura 76. verse 12-21). They will also be provided with companions of chaste maidens untouched by any man or jinn (Sura 55. verse 56, Sura56. verse 22 and Sura 78. verse 33). There also is the river Kausar whose water is sweeter than honey, whiter than milk. It smells sweeter than musk. He who drinks of its water shall never thirst. "Lo! whose cometh guilty unto his Lord, Verily for him is hell. There he will neither die nor live " (Sura XX, verse 74)

And Hell, the Traditionalist observes has also seven zones. In the first zone (Jahannam) the sinned Muslims will be punished and in the last, the hypocrites and false Prophets. The people of the Book, the idolaters and Polytheists will suffer punishment in the remaining five zones. The chief weapon of punishment is Fire (Al-Nar) and Quran describes in many suras the severity of the hell-fire. It is "a raging fire, and food which choketh (the partaker) and a painful doom" (Sura 73.12). The erring and deniers be given in Hell boiling water to drink.

(Sura 38.57) (Sura LVI.54 and Sura 37. verse 67) and they will drink like a camel drinks water. They will be given fruit of the tree of Zaqqum to eat (Sura 37. verse 62. Sura XLIV. verse 43 and Sura LVI. verse 52) and they will fill their bellies with these bitter fruits. In the literature on Miraj, it is given that the Prophet has seen the fire in hell when Malik opened the lid, out of fear, he immediately requested him to close it. However, the punishment in hell seems to be very severe. Instead of water to quench the thirst, they will be given stinking water and liquids that are boiling. This adds misery to them. Virtually, they will be roasted in the infernal fire.

The contemporary writers[1] say that the Paradise and Hell as described in the Holy Books are not limited to a particular place but show two conditions of life. In the former the soul attains the perfection and in the latter, the soul is destorted and stunted. Viewed against this perspective, heaven and hell are the two evolutionary stages of the soul's journey in the realms beyond grave. The soul of a just man becomes blessed and lives in communion with God for ever. On the contrary, the condemned soul is damned and suffers for ever in hell. The philosophers disagree with the orthodox interpretation, and deny the possibility of any resurrection of the body in the Last Day. According to the philosophic interpretation, the punishment and reward will be mental and spiritual and defenitely not bodily. It also interprets God's seeing, sitting etc. as allegoric representation for His Knowledge, Power etc. The orthodox considers the Throne made of His Light and the Chair attached to the throne. There are four rivers round the throne—one consisting of pearls, another of fire, third of white snow and the last of water. The vastness of The Throne is incomparable. When compared to the throne, the chair is like a ring in a desert.

This thinking pulls down the entire structure of the vast literature built on the delights of heaven and torments of hell. They are mere figuritive expressions and should be treated as such.

VI. BELIEF IN PREDESTINATION

Allah has predestined every thing including the eternal fate of man and this absolute predestination or eternal decree (Kadar) is an article of

---

[1]Kwaja Kamaluddin's, *The Ideal Prophet*, especially pp. 107-108. The Working Mission, London 1925.

belief. It is based on the Quranic preaching that, "all things have been created after fixed decree." (Sura LIV.49). There is another passage in Quran (Sura VII. verse 178) "He who Allah leadeth indeed is led aright, while he whom Allah sendeth astray—they indeed are losers." It is related from Abdulla ibn Umar that" the Apostle of Allah said,'God wrote the fate of all creation fifty thousand years before He created the heavens and the earth ' "(Muslim)[1]. This affirms the orthodox belief that everything good and bad proceed from the Divine Will. Everything is fixed and recorded on a preserved tablet. In other words, it is a total and complete denial of free will of man.

The Kadarites[2] refused to swallow the creed of predestination as believed by the Orthodox. They argued that if a man acts according to divine commands, there is no point in punishing or rewarding him for the bad or good deeds of his own actions. So he must be responsible for his own actions. In other words, man is the creator so far as his own actions are concerned. The Traditionalists oppose it for the simple reason that God is the only creator. A new path was opened by the Kadarites which was later taken over by the Mutazilites.

Applying reason to the beliefs, this group broke away from the traditionalists and stood as Mutazilities (Secession). Like Kadarites, they put reason into the idea of predestination and found that man and man alone is responsible for his acts. They opposed Predestination vehemently. As man is responsible for the sin he commits, they advocated severe punishment to the sinner, as against the belief of the orthodoxy. Another Mutazilites teaching which opposes Orthodox Islamic teaching is that punishment in Hell is everlasting, and those who enter Hell will never be delivered from it. On the contrary, the common belief among the Muslims is that those having faith, even though they have committed grave sins, will be brought back to heaven. In fact torments of Hell for them are only momentary. Not satisfied with this, they raised objections in the various Qualities (Sifat) of God, such as Knowledge, Power, Life, for these Qualities appear to be separate Beings as against the Unity of God. Godhead is indivisible. On the contrary these Qual-

---

[1] Selection from Muhammadan Tradition. p. 7

[2] It is a misnomer that, the sect who disbelieve the eternal decree was known as Kadarites. They are a minority of Karijites. The founder of Kadarite doctrine is Ma'bah al-Juhani (death 80 A.H.) of Basra. As they believe in the creative Power of God and that of Man, they are also called Dualists of the Community.

ities make Him separate Beings. Further, analysing the Traditionalist interpretation of Quranic verses that the Believers will see God seated in the Throne (Istawa) and that God, after Heavens and earth were created mounted the Throne (Sura LVII.4, Sura XX.5) the Mutazilities argued that these make God limited whereas He is unlimited. Otherwise, how can he be seated in a throne. Similarly, they did not wait long to reject the orthodox-Quran-Commentary of God having hands [1] and eyes [2] like any one of us have organs of sight, hearing etc. They argued that they are all symbolic representation and they should be understood as such. The Mutazilites also scoff at the idea that Allah will be seen by some of His Believers. They even quoted fragments of Scriptures, disprove the commentaries of the Traditionalists. Sura II. 286 is quoted in Support of their belief. "Allah does not charge a soul with more than it can bear. It shall be requited for whatever good and whatever evil it has done."

Again Sura IV. 40: "Lo! Allah wrongeth not any one even the weight of an ant: and if it be a good action, he wili double it, and will recompense it in his sight with a great reward."

The result is that Mutazilite advocated severe punishment for wrong doers. Fortune and support came and gone for the Mutazilite. They were condemned, and praised. But in the end the orthodox seemed to be holding the trump card and well in time they played it too. The orthodox disposed of the rationalism of the Mutazilite by two words, "Bila Kayfa". (Believe without asking how). They further said that Allah's eyes mean the Power of Seeing all things and His hands mean the effectual Nature of His energy and must not be understood anthropomorphically. Whatever be the merits and demerits of the Mutazilite thinking, they brought rationalism in Islam and judged the people on the basis of good or bad works they had performed. This, in a way helped them to shed away the laziness and mental snobbishness that threatened orthodox Islam.

The fortune of the Mutazilite came when Al-Mamun ascended the

---

[1] Sura XXIII.88 say: In whose *hand* is the dominion over all things.
Sura XXXVI.82. Therefore glory be to Him in whose *hand* is the dominion over all things.

[2] Sura XI. 37 & XXIII. 27: Build your ship under Our *Eyes* and by Our inspiration
Sura LII. 48. "So wait patiently for thy Lord's decree for surely thou art in Our *sight*."
Sura LIV. 14 "That run (upon the waters) in Our sight."

throne of Islamic Empire. He did not wait long to announce his approval of the Mutazilite dogma. He had gone to the extent of making a state declaration that Quran was created. With rigorous penalty for non-believer of the state order, he imposed it to his unwilling subjects. Not long, the Mutazilite met their worst opponent in Ahmad ibn Hanbal who in spite of stiff opposition from the ruler stood firm on his ground. He said that theology and reasoning would never go together. For openly opposing the Mutazilites, he was harassed, tortured and even imprisoned, but he stuck to his gun. After his death, his pupils continued the teaching of their master which had such an influence among the masses that ultra Hanbalites compared things in God with those of His creature.

That is Face of God, His Feet and Limbs, His eyes, Ears all resemble those of men. The other great name who opposed the Mutazilites tooth and nail was Shaikh Abul Hasan al-Ashari. He had to meet two strong opposition, Mutazilities and Hanbalites. The latter even called him 'infidel' but the Traditionalists supported him. Al-Ashari upheld seven rational qualities of God (Sifat Aqliya)—Life, knowledge, Power, Will, Hearing, Seeing and Speech. Like Malik ibn Anas, Al-Ashari met the Mutazilite opposition for anthropomorphism in God by asking them to believe without asking how (Bila Kayfa). Later he went a step further and said that things in God were incomparable. That is he said, "Bila Kayfa Wala Tashbih" (believe without asking how and without any comparision). He settled the argument of free-will by adopting a middle path. He combined the free-will of the Mutazilite with the Predestination of the Orthodox Islam. God, he said, is the only creator. He creates Power (Qadar) and Choice (Ikhtiyar). Then God creates in man actions. So the man is the subject of the Action already created by God.

Studying every passage in the Quran with reference to the circumstances necessitating its revelation, Dr. Syed Muzaffaruddin Nadvi in his book, '*Muslim Thought and Its Sources*' observes that "the only right conclusion we arrive at is that God is undoubtedly the supreme Sovereign, with very wide powers, but that human beings also have some hand in moulding their destiny, in as much as they can make choice between good and evil, right and wrong. Whenever God speaks of predestination or pre-arrangement of human affairs, He generally means that they must conform to the usual course of action, i.e., the law of nature. Man, within the limited sphere of his existence, is a builder of his character and an architect of his fortune, subject to the control and supervision of the supreme Intelligence."[1]

[1]*Muslim Thought and Its Source*, by Syed Muzzaffar-ud-Din Nadvi Lahore 1946 pp. 14-16 (Requoted from *Studies in Muslim Ethics* by Dwight M. Donaldson) pp. 24-25, London 1953.

4. PILLARS OF ISLAM

Islam is a religion of practices consisting of (1) the recitation of the confession of faith and serving God without associating anything with Him, (2) in performing the ritual prayer, (3) in giving legal alms, (4) in fasting during the month of Ramadan, and (5) visiting al-Kaba in pilgrimage in the month of Dul-Haj. These five duties are the real foundations of Islam. Known as the Pillars of Islam (Arkan Al-din) they are obligatory to every believer. Its performance makes a Mumin a Muslim and is a Fard Ayn. And obviously its non-performance is a sin punishable. To a query, "What is Islam?" by Gabriel disguised in the robe of a man and appeared before the Prophet when he was sitting with Umar and some other companions of the Prophet, he said,"Islam is that thou bear witness that there is no God but Allah, and that Muhammad is the Apostle of Allah (Shahadat) and that thou observe prayer (Salat) and that thou give alms (Zakat) and that thou keep the fast in the month of Ramadan (Saum) and that thou make the pilgrimage to the House (i.e. the temple[1] at Mecca) if thou art able to provide for the journey (Haj)."[2]

The sequence of the religious duties (Ibadat) is important and fixed. There is a Tradition related by Ibn Umar [3] and approved by Imam Bukhari, the great scholar and compiler of Hadith that observance of Saum becomes the fifth duty. First is belief in the Absolute Unity of God, (secondly) obedience to Him i.e., worship, (thirdly) one's responsibility to the Community of Believers (alms giving), (fourthly) one's acts of self purification (fast) and (finally) a visit to the Sacred City of Mecca (Pilgrimage). It is said that a certain man once made an attempt to interchange fast in the month of Ramadan with alms giving. Thereupon, Umar said, "No, first the fast of Ramadan, then the pilgrimage so I have heard it from the mouth of Muhammad." There is another popular story also recorded on the authority of Umar. It is related that Umar witnessed that the Prophet replied a man thus: "Islam is wit-

---

[1]Temple is misnomer. Mosque at Mecca.

[2] Selections from Muhammadan Tradition by Rev. W. Goldsack.

[3] In another Hadith Ibn Umar relates the sequence as above i.e., Shahadat, Salat, Zakat, Saum and Haj.

nessing that there is no God but Allah, and that Muhammad is the Apostle of Allah, performing the Salat, handing over the Zakat, fasting during Ramadan, and the pilgrimage if there be no hindrance." No Believer is exempted from the acceptance of Shahadat i.e., indivisibility of Godhead and the Apostleship of Muhammad. In fact, confession of Shahadat separates Believer from non-believers. Irrespective of sex, age or social status, no Muslim is exempted from Shahadat under any circumstance. Next is the observance of the ritual Salat. Exempted are women during menstruation. Even the sick, and travellers have to perform the worship. Zakat, a kind of tax on one's possession is obligatory for those who possess wealth. From observance of Fasting, sick persons, travellers and nursing mothers are exempted. Pilgrimage to Mecca, the fifth Pillars of Islam is compulsory only for the rich, for those who can afford the expense for the journey. In practice, it excludes most of the Believers.

This leads us to the consideration of the spiritual importance of the religious duties. Shahadat is the confession and acknowledgement of the existence of the Only One God. It is the Central Pillar on which the edifice of Islam is built. Acceptance of Shahadat is the only condition, Islam prescribes for the converts to its uncompromising monotheism. Thus, with a frank acceptance and recitation of the article of Faith, Islam dispenses with a hundred formalities and rituals of conVersion. Next in importance is rituals Salat. Worship is obedience as that of a servant (Abd) to his lord. Zakat, the third duty of a Muslim prepares him to be responsive of the requirements of the Community as a whole. It inculcates in him, the idea of Brotherhood, and love to fellow beings. Fourth is Saum or Fasting. Saum in the ninth month of the Islamic calendar is a sort of soul exercise by attempting to control all vices. Fasting trains the fasters as good disciplinarians both physically and spiritually. Haj, the last duty prescribed to the votaries of Islam prepares the participants to sacrifice the wordly comforts for the way of God. That may be preparing for a visit to the cradle of Islam for their whole lives, planning for it, dreaming it in every sleep. They might be performing worship and distributing alms and fasting all the prescribed fasts and more before they finally set out for the Pilgrimage. With the completion of Haj, they come back as an example unto themselves.

There is a tradition approved as genuine by Imam Muslim is as follows: "Once there came to the Apostle of Allah a man from the people of Najd with dishevelled hair; we heard the humming of his voice, but we did not understand what he said till he was near the Apostle of Allah. Then he began to ask him about Islam. The Apostle of Allah answered: Five Salats every day and night. He asked: No more? The Prophet answered: No, what is above this number, is supererogatory. Further, the fast of Ramadan. He asked: No more? The Prophet answered: No, what is more than that, is supererogatory. Further, the Apostle of Allah mentioned the Zakat. No, what is above it, is supererogatory. Thereupon the man went away saying: By Allah, I shall add nothing, nor omit anything. Then the Apostle of Allah said: "He is saved, if he keeps his promise."[1] So the religious duties enjoined upon the followers of Islam are broadly classified into two—obligatory and voluntary. Salat (Liturgical worships five times daily), Zakat (alms-giving) Saum (Fasting) during Ramadan and annual Haj (Pilgrimage) are the obligatory duties. Supererogatory worships, Sadka (voluntary alms-giving), fasting especially in Muharram etc. and Umra or lesser pilgrimage are the voluntary duties whose performances and observance are recommended and rewarded but whose omissions are not punishable. On the contrary non-performance of any of the obligatory duties is punishable.

Now let us consider in detail the cardinal duties obligatory to the followers of Islam.

FIRST PILLAR OF ISLAM

Shahadat

Islamic Creed is shortened into two statements and both of them together is called Kalimatu sh-Shahadah. It is popularly known as Kalimah, literally meaning "The Word". The witnessing, that is acceptance and recital of the Kalimah that *La ilah illa Allah: Muhammadan Rasulu Allah"* (There is no God but Allah and Muhammad is the Messenger of Allah) is the first of the five Foundations or Pillars of Islam. It is the creed in brief. The creed proper is *Ash-Hadu An La ilah Allah, Wa Ashh Hadu Anna Muhammadun Rasulu Allah—I testify that there is no God* but Allah, and I testify that Muhammad is the Messenger of Allah. Reciting the Shahadat is called Tashahud and is an important rite of the Islamic worship. Thus, the Believers recite it in every worship. Any one who believes and confesses the Kalimah, by virtue of the acceptance of the faith becomes a Believer. This easy acceptance of the Faith is claimed

[1]Requoted from The Muslim Creed A.J. Wensinck. p. 21. London Cambridge 1932.

as one of the distinct advantages of Islam. It is not the birth, family status or wealth of a person or any ritual confession that determine faith or Din, but the confession of the Unity of God and the Apostleship of Muhammad that makes him a Muslim. In this way Islamic doctrine is simple, direct, frank and universal. Only a confession of the Kalimah is what one requires. The moment the creed is confessed with the tongue, believed with the mind and known with the heart, he becomes a Muslim, pure and simple. But however the orthodox strongly favours public confession of faith with lips. On the contrary, the Murjites[1] held that faith is a confession in the heart and is a private intercourse with God and so public confession is not needed. In other words, Murjites doctrine allows a Jew and a Christian to be a Believer (Mumin) of the faith inwardly despite the fact that they believe in the testimony without any outward utterance. That is, a person can be a believer (Momin) inwardly while appearing to be a non-Muslim outwardly. Further, the Murjites believed that faith in God and His Apostle will protect a person from the torments of hell, and faith will never increase or decrease. Emphasising on the Goodness, Mercy and Love of God to His creatures, the Murjites cast doubt of the eternal punishment to the Believers. To them, God is the only true Judge of human actions. In accordance with this belief, they do not mind to wait till the Last Day to hear the judgement of God. Later led by Abu Hanifa, some of the Murjites held that faith is "acknowledgement with the tongue as well as the heart and that works are a necessary supplement." His thinking comes quite close to the orthodox view.

The six conditions prescribed for confession are :

1. Saying the Kalimah aloud at least once in life-time
2. Understand it clearly and fully,
3. Believe it by the heart,
4. Profess it until death,
5. Recite it correctly, and
6. Profess and declare it without hesitation.

Eventhough elements of Shahadah occur throughout the Sacred Text[2] the Sayings of the Messenger are the forerunners of Kalimah.

---

[1]Murjites, a sect of Islam formed out of the civil war between the Shiites, Kharijites and the Umayyads.

[2]References in Quran of the Unity of God.

Sura II.256. Ayatul Kursi (Verse of Throne)

Allah! There is no God save Him, the Alive, the Eternal

(Contd....)

He used to say,"Islam is external, faith belongs to the heart." In the literature of the Prophet's Night Journey to Jerusalem and ascent to heaven and final admittance to the Presence of Allah, it is said, the Prophet whirling off the House of Adoration, he passed through a region of dazzling light and inky darkness until he was only two bow shots away from the Throne of God. There he saw the glory of the face of God and the words, "La ilah illa Allah: Muhammad Rasul Allah" glittering on the right side of God's throne.

Kalimah is designed as the religious summary of Islam which is to be used by its adherents. Having two leading principles of Islam, Monotheism and Apostleship of Muhammad, it is the simplest of all creeds. The common man does not bother much about the subteleties of faith; he simply accepts and confesses the Kalimah. The first testimony that "La ilah illa Allah" affirms the faith in the Absolute Unity of God or Tawhid and the second, "Muhammadun Rasulu Allah" in the Apostleship of Muhammad.

The first principle is called Nafi Wa Isbat. It preaches the monotheism of Islam. It is the witnessing of the Unity of God (Tawhid). God is One. He is the only Creator and Sustainer. He has no Partner, no

---

Neither slumber nor sleep overtaketh him. Unto Him belongeth whatsoever is in the heavens and whatever is in the earth........"

Sura CXII. "Say: He is Allah, the One!
Allah, the eternity Besought of all!
He begetteth not nor was begotten
And there is none comparable unto Him."

Sura XXVIII.88" And cry not unto any other God along with Allah. There is no God Save Him.
Every thing will perish save his countenance,
His is the command, and unto Him ye will be brought back."

Sura XLVII.19
"So know that there is no God save Allah _______"

References in Quran of the Apostleship of Muhammad
"Muhammad is the Messenger of Allah"

Combined references in Quran of the Unity of God and Apostleship of Muhammad
Sura VII. 158 "Say: O mankind! Lo! I am the messenger of Allah to you all __ (the Messenger of) Him unto whom belongeth the sovereignty of the heavens and the earth. There is no God save Him. He quickeneth and He giveth death. So believe in Allah and His messenger, the Prophet who can neither read nor write who believeth in Allah and in His words and follow him that
happily ye may be led aright."

Equal, no Rival. He is Omnipresent and Omniscient. He is all the Seer, all the Hearer, all the Knower. He is the most Mighty, the most Powerful, the most Merciful and the most Compassionate. It is this expression, the expression of Absolute Unity and Indivisibility of God that was preached by all the prophets. So all those who believe in the first part of Kalimah are Muslims. Above all, those who believe in One God, perhaps Jews, Christians etc. are Muslims.

Nafi wa Isbat has two statements, one of rejection called Nafi (that which is rejected) and the other of acceptance, Isbat (that which is established). The first phrase that 'there is no God' (La ilah) is an outright denial, and rejection of all Gods, and the second,"but Allah" (Illa Allah) is an affirmation of the existence of the Only One God. By expression of this phrase, the Unity of God, His Absolute Power and His Essential Attributes of an Eternal and Almighty Being are believed, accepted and confessed.

The second principle of Kalimah is witnessing that Muhammad is the Messenger of Allah (Muhammadun Rasul Allah). He accepts and confirms the Apostleship of Muhammad. It is here that Islam differs from Judaism and Christianity. Jews believe all Prophets of Old Testament from Adam to Noah, Abraham and Moses. Christians believe all Prophets of Old Testament and New Testament from Adam upto Jesus, and Muslims believe in all Prophets upto Jesus, and Muhammad. To brief, Jews disbelieve in the Apostleship of Jesus and Muhammad, Christians refuse to recognise the messengership in Muhammad but Muslims believe as an article of faith in all the prophets mentioned in the Testaments and Muhammad. Those who believe in the first and second testimonies are Mumins (the Faithful). Obviously, belief in the second part alone is impossible as it is an off shoot of the first testimony. This testimony also indirectly makes one to believe in all the heaven-sent Apostles from Adam to Muhammad. The Tradition records about 1,24,000 Prophets and 315 Apostles, and nine of them are special messengers (Ulul Azm). They are Noah, Abraham, David, Jacob, Joseph, Job, Moses, Jesus and Muhammad. Six of the Prophets have special titles: Adam (Safiyu llah, The Chosen of God), Noah (Nabiyu 'llah, the Preacher of God), Abraham (Khalilu 'llah, the Friend of God), Moses (Kalimu 'llah, the Converser with God), Jesus (Ruhu 'llah, the Spirit of God), and Muhammad (Rasulu 'llah, the Messenger of God). The full information of Messengership of Muhammad occurs in the following Suras) Sura XLVIII.29, XLIII.45, LXI.5, XXXIII.40, VII.157, II.285 and IV.135).

Indirectly, the second part of Kalimah proves Muhammad's excellence over the rest of the Prophets. It makes us believe that the Apostleship of God begins with Adam passing through many Prophets to culminate in the final Apostleship of Muhammad.

SECOND PILLAR OF ISLAM

Salat or Prayer

Prayer is the key to paradise and is the first duty of a Muslim. In fact, it is the most important devotional exercise in Islam. Revered as the second Pillar of religion, it is so important that the Prophet said,"the most evil of mankind is the one who steals from his prayer." The review of a person's works on the judgement Day begins with prayer. If he has performed them well, he will be saved. Of the many forms of prayer, eight are important. (Imam Ghazali)[1] They are Salat or Worship, al-Tilawa (the Recital of the Quran), al-Du'a (the offering of Supplication), al-Dhikr (the invocation of the names of Allah and mentioning His Qualities), al-Wird (the Recital of a section of the Quran or other religious works), al-Hizb (making petition using a portion of the Quran or other devotional writing), Itikalf (retreat within a mosque for offering prayers and Supplication),Mawlid (celebration of the birthday of the Prophet and Muslim Saints) and Ziyara (visit to Tombs of saints).[2] Even though observance of prayer in general is meritorious, few of them have special rewards. Some are obligatory; others are recommended or voluntary. Salat is obligatory and is made incumbent on every Muslim who attains puberty and is of sound mind. It is so important a religious duty, the early theologian did not even refuse to consider those who neglected Salat as infidels. Faith is better than prayer because faith is continuous whereas prayer consists of five-times-a-day performance only. Faith can not be postponed on any circumstances. On the contrary prayer can be temporarily suspended on valid reasons. Similarly, faith without prayer is beneficial whereas prayer without faith has little benefit.

Salat[3]. The word Salat is thought to be derived from 'Salawa'. Salat also means Du'a (Supplication) which is an important act of Islamic ceremonial prayer. Hence, the whole devotional exercise is called Salat

---

[1] Abdul Hamid Muhammad ibn Muhammad ibn Muhammad al-Ghazali. (A.H 1058-1111)

[2] Wahabis object to this.

[3] Plural Salawat.

or Worship. Literally Salat means inclination. In its technical meaning, it is the ceremonial or liturgical prayer, comprising of Invocation, Recital and Supplication on Standing, Bowing, Prostration and Sitting. Salat is not merely an external act. There must be an inner urge—the urge of the soul to perform the worship. The mere act of worship does not bring spiritual awakening.

It is related that the Prophet said, "How many standing up will have as their portion from their worship only fatigue and misfortune."[1] Worship in Islam is a combination of physical and spiritual urge, it is a harmonious blending of belief and action. The belief that God is one is expressed in words and the prayer stands in complete submission to the Will of God. As a matter of fact, Salat is nothing but a sincere and successful attempt of a man as a humble creature in direct communion with his Lord without least helped (or exploited) by a mediator. He stands alone before Him and alone he offers his Supplication and Invocation. In this aspect Islamic Worship is unique. It shows man a direct approach to his creator.

Opinions differ on the status of a person who neglects the worship. Most of the Ulamas[2] say a neglector of worship (Tarik Al-Salat) is a Fasik.[3] It is said by others that such a neglector is an infidel[4]. (This term infidel or Kafir is different from Mushrikin or Associators i.e., those who associate another God with Allah.)

The essential elements of Salat are humbleness and Presence of heart. Humbleness is a sign of obedience, humility and submission to the Divine Will. It is indeed the wholehearted admission of the Essence of God, His Attributes and Qualificatives. Every act, every movement, every utterance in Salat is a sign of this admission. By the first act of worship, that is Standing in obedience before God, the Prayer recognises the absolute indivisibility of God, His Will, His Power and His Knowledge. Obedience also recognises the Qualificatives of God that is Seeing, Hearing, Speaking etc. The second act in Worship is Inclination or Bowing which is an act of humility; and Prostration, the last act is submission and surrender to the Divine Will, obviously develops the human faculties. Primarily, this inculcates in the Worshipper, a sense of love for fellow human beings. It cultivates in him the idea of Broth-

---

[1] Worship in Islam. Al-Ghazali Translated by Calverley pp. 86-87.

[2] As-Shaffi, Malik.

[3] There by his faith is not decreased. It is caused because of a fault of behaviour.,

[4] Ahmad ibn Hanbal.

erhood and Oneness. The environment of a Worship-mat is congenial for inculcating this sense of love, brotherhood and Oneness, especially in an Islamic Congregational Worship, the Muslims, both high and low stand shoulder to shoulder before the One and Only God, that even after they disperse, this feeling of unity prevails in the minds of the participants for ever. Peace with fellow beings is one of the pre-requisites of Islamic prayers. It begins with the ejaculation Allah Akbar i.e., God is Great and ends with a Salutation of Peace i.e., Saying peace on either side. This is the formal beginning and formal ending of Islamic Prayer. Peace with others cannot be maintained unless one becomes good inwardly and outwardly. Good works alone open the gates of spiritual awakening. Whosoever inculcates peace with fellow-beings and does good deeds to mankind, "his reward is with his Lord; and there shall no fear come upon him neither shall he grieve." (Sura II. 112).

Presence of heart is the essence of Salat. His actions should coincide with his utterances. The Prophet said, "Allah does not look at the worship in which a man does not present his heart along with his body." This is possible only when he fully realises and understands each and every word he utters. In order to understand fully the meanings of every word, the Worshipper must have knowledge of the Scripts. If the worshipper prays with an empty heart and fails to understand the meanings of his utterances, the worships of such a person will not lift him to spiritual perfectness. To cite an example, if the worshipper is unfamiliar with the ninety-nine excellent names of God, he fails to understand The Glorious and Terrible Attributes of God, the vast differences of these titles and the various qualificatives and attributes of God. In other words, he misses the very essence of God. God is Ar-Rahman (The Merciful) and Ar-Rahim (The Compassionate); He is Al-Aziz (The Mighty) and Al-Ghafur (The Forgiving); He is Al-Khaliq (The Creator) and Al-Muzil (The Destroyer); He is Al-Haqq (The Truthful) and Al-Hakeem (The Wise); He is As-Sami (The Hearer) and Al-Basir (The Seer); He is Al-Awwal (The First) and Al-Akhir (The Last). Unfortunately, many of the devout Muslims observe the letter of the religious law but fail to enquire into its meaning. Indeed, what they do are not more than physical exercises without any insight into the inner meaning. Or, they lack the inner urge. Al-Quran itself is severe to them. It states, "Draw not near into prayer when you are drunken[1] till ye

[1] Intoxication as a result of drinking has been recently interpreted in a figuritive meaning. It means intoxication on account of excessive prayers. As such any one who is in a state of being constant in prayer need no canonical worship. A fish in the sea

know that which ye utter, nor when ye are pollutted, save when journeying upon the road, till ye have bathed." (Sura IV. Verse 43). Unmindful or mere forgetfulness in Salat invalidates the entire worship. The presence of mind in Islamic Worship is so unavoidably important that one day the Prophet disagreed to have new straps in his sandal on account of its fancy and new look. At once he discarded the straps. One another occasion, he presented a pair of new chappals to a poor man on similar grounds. He also threw away a ring from his hand as he looked at it repeatedly while delivering a sermon.

Worship with heart fully engaged in worldly affairs has no meaning and it completely defeats the very purpose of devotion. So, it is even recommended to perform the night worship after taking night meal so that the heart will be free of any engagement. Similarly, it is recommended that during Ramadan the breaking of the Fast should precede the sunset Worship so that the pangs of hunger and thirst should not engage the worshipper from offering a true and sincere invocation.

CONGREGATIONAL WORSHIP AND INDIVIDUAL WORSHIP

Islam recognises congregational worship as well as individual worship. Both have excellence of their own, but group worship, as it inculcates Brotherhood is preferred and has greater reward. A Prophetic Saying that 'Worship in the congregation is more excellent than Worship alone by twenty seven degrees' shows the excellence of congregational Worship. For this matter, Friday Noon Worship, popularly known as Juma Prayer is par excellence. Usually, the Congregational worship is held in a mosque except those performed in connection with the two festivals (Id al Fitr and Id al Adha) and Worship for request for rain. Individual worship may be performed in any clean place, open or closed. The latter is preferred on account of its privacy so that scattering away of thoughts can be minimised. In order to limit the range of vision, the devotees prefer to worship leaving just enough space for prostration. In the first years of Islam, the pious even preferred dark rooms. Regarding the excellence of individual worship in one's house, the Prophet is related to have said, "Worship in this mosque (al-medina) is

---

needs no bathing. For details see Understanding Islam by Frithjof Schuon, Translation by D.M. Matheson. p.27

more excellent than a thousand performances of worship in any other Mosque, and worship in the inviolate mosque (at Mecca) is more excellent than a thousand performances of the worship in my mosque and, more excellent than all that, is the worship of a man who performs in the corner of his house a worship of two raka's that no one knows about except Allah."

PRIVATE PRAYER (DU'A) AND RITUAL WORSHIP (SALAT)

Private prayer in Islam is Du'a. Having no regulation, the utterances can be made in any language the prayer wishes to be. On the contrary, ritual or canonical worship is Salat and must be said in Arabic only. Probably, this is one of the strong reasons which inculcates unity and Brotherhood among Muslims. The Chinese, Indians, Africans, Persians, Arabs, all Muslims which ever country they belong say their ritual worship in one common language, that is Arabic. Undoubtedly, Arabic is the only language, such a vast number of people from almost all races from many countries of the world use for ritual worship.

Considering its importance, Salat is classified into two, Fard and Nafl.

Fard

The liturgical worships prescribed in Al-Quran are Fard. These are the five daily performances----Dawn (Fajr having two Rak'as)[1], Noon (Zuhr, 4 Rak'as), mid-afternoon (Asr, 4 Rak'as), Sunset (Mag'arib, 3 Rak'as) and Night (Isha, 4 Rak'as). Their observance in the appointed times is compulsory for every Muslim who has attained puberty and has the capacity to use reason. However, women in menstruation and in convalescene from child birth are exempted. The intentional omission is a sin, unpardonable. But however omission because of some unavoidable work is to be made up.

Hours of Worship[2]

Islamic calendar is lunar and the month begins with the visibility of the moon. That is, the first hour of the day begins with the first hour after the appearence of the moon (corresponding to roughly eighteen

---

[1]A cycle of prayer from the Takbir of a standing Posture to the Takbir of the next Standing Posture.

[2]There is a difference of opinion between the various schools.

hours.) So the first worship of the day is **Maghrib** (Sunset). The time to perform **Maghrib** is the brief period between the sunset(actual disappearance of the sun in the western horizon) and the disappearance of the red glow from the sky. **Isha** is the second worship to be performed any time in the night between the disappearance of the red glow of the sunset and midnight. Next is **Fajr**. The time of performance is between the true dawn (Day break) and the sunrise. The time for **Zuhr** the fourth canonical worship is when the sun begins to decline at midday until the shadow of any object is equal in length to the object itself. The time of **Asr,** the fifth and the last worship is midway between Zuhr and Magharib, that is, from the end of the time of Zuhr unitl the time when the sun turns yellow.

The number and time of the liturgical worships are mainly based on the traditional precepts of the Prophet. Let us trace it in the literature of Tradition. It is related that when the Prophet was admitted in the presence of Allah on the Night of power,[1] God's injunctions were that the followers of Muhammad should worship fifty times a day, and Muhammad reached the seventh heaven on his return journey was met by Moses[2] who enquired,"What have you been ordered?" The Prophet said,"Fifty worships daily." Then Moses said,"Verily your followers will not be able to perform fifty worships every day; and verily, I swear by Allah, that I tried the experiment with men before you, and applied a remedy to the sour of Israel, but without the desired effect; then return to your Lord, and ask that the load of your followers may be lightened." Thereupon, the Prophet returned to the Divine Presence. God, so goes the Traditional Literature, was pleased to reduce it by ten.[3] Moses again voiced concern in forty daily worships. Muhammad returned a second time. Ten more worships were taken away. Moses again became doubtful in thirty performances and persuaded Muhammad to go back to the presence of God for further concessions. God's bounty is unlimited. The burden of ten more worships was reduced. But Moses again doubted in twenty worships and Muhammad returned to God's court until the number was fixed at five. It is surprising to note that nowhere in the Script, the five daily worships are mentioned. However, the passage coming near to the Tradition runs thus: "Glorify God when it is evening,

---

[1] The journey of the Prophet to Jerusalem and from there his ascent to Heaven.

[2] Commentators disagree. Some say Muhammad met Abraham.

[3] Katadan and Ibani Shahab state that each time 10 worships were reduced but Sabit says that each time only 5 worships were lessened.

and at morning, and to Him be praise in the heavens and earth, and at afternoon and at noontime." (Sura XXX. The Romans. verses 17-18) Quran commentators interpret that the evening worship includes both the worships before sunset and after and hence it goes well with the Tradition. However, the sacred text enjoins the Muslims to be constant at the stated prayers and it is repeated in not less than forty six times.

	Sura	No. of Times
II	Cow	5
IV	Women	4
V	The Table	3
VI	Cattle	1
VII	Al Araf	1
VIII	Spoils	1
IX	Immunity	5
XI	Hud	2
XIII	Thunder	1
XIV	Abraham	1
XVII	The Night Journey	1
XIX	Mary	2
XX	Ta-Ha	2
XXII	Pilgrimage	2
XXIII	True Believer	1
XXIV	Light	2
XXIV	The Ant	1
XXIX	The Spider	1
XXX	The Greeks	2*
XXXI	Lokman	1
XXXIII	The Confederate	1
XXXV	The Creator	1
XL	The True Believer	1
L	Qaf	1
LXII	The Assembly	1
LXXIII	The Hypocrite	1
LXXV	Recreation	1
		46**

* 5—time Prayer intended in one of these Passages.

** In combination with Alms giving, it occurs in few more suras.

The Prophet is related to have said," The five performances of the worship are like a river, fresh and deep, beside the door of any of you, into which he plunges five times everyday, and what do you think that leaves of his uncleanness?"

His companions replied, "Not anything!"

He said,"so the five performances of the worship remove offences as water removes dirt."[1]

Fard worship is so important that non-observance of even one of them is punishable. However three modifications are allowed on special grounds.

1. A traveller may perform two rak'as instead of the usual four rak'as in the noon, afternoon and night worships.
2. Similarly a traveller may combine noon worship with that of afternoon, and the sunset with the night worships.
3. In fear as in a battle field, or running from fire and wild beast, it is allowed to worship on foot or on riding. Facing the Ka'ba (Qibla) is not obligatory on these occasions. It is however a recommendation. On the contrary, he can pray facing any direction. Similarly, he is exempted from bowing and prostration. Instead, a mere nodding of the head is enough.

Nafl (Supererogatory)[2]

Literally Nafl means additional and so, all worships not prescribed and are based on the worships performed by the Prophet are Nafl or supererogatory. Omission of any or all of them is not punishable; but observing them is good and has a reward. Each of them has excellence of its own. Of the Nafl, the Congregational worship of the two feasts—Id al Fitr and Id al Adha—are the most excellent followed by the worship of the Eclipse of the Sun. Of the individual Nafl, the Witr Salat is the most meritorious, then the two Rak'a worship before the Fard worship. Nafl worships are classified according to the excellence. According to the former calculation they are divided into three—Sunna (Usage or Customary Worship), Mustahabb (Liked Worship), and Tatawwu (Voluntary).

Salat As-Sunna are mostly confirmed congregational worships observed by the Prophet and omitted by him on strong reasons. On the

[1]Worship in Islam. p. 43.

[1]Singular Nafila.

sons. On the contrary, the worships performed by the Prophet sometimes are Mustahabb. Performance of Mustahabb is 'Liked'. Tatawwu are voluntary worships performed by the Prophet on the general basis that all worships are good, and their observance as much as possible has reward.

Nafl worship according to the time of performance are four— Daily, Weekly, Yearly and Occasional.

1 Daily Supererogatory

There are eight worships recommended to be performed daily, five before and after the Fard or Liturgical worships called Ratiba and three others, Witr (Odd), Duha (Forenoon) and Ihya (Enlivening) worships before the liturgical worships make the mind more receptive for communion with God. That performed after the Prescribed Salat has the merit of making up any deficiency or omission in the earlier worship. The hours to perform the Five Ratiba worship are in the early morning before the Salatul Fadr, in the noon (six Rak'a worship, 4 before and 2 Rak'a after Zuhr), Mid afternoon (4 rak'a before salatul Asr), Sunset (2 Rak'a after Salatul Maghrib), Mid aftrnoon (4 Rak's after Salatul Isha). The Witr is a worship with odd Rak'as (1,3,5,7 etc.) performed any time after sunset but before the Day break worship. There is a difference of opinion whether it can be connected with a Fard worship or not. However, it seems good if it is performed unconnected. The number of rak'as the Prophet had prayed or Witr also seems to have been disputed. He had prayed upto 13 to 17 rak'as. Duha is performed any time in the early, mid or late afternoon, the number of rak'as being four, six or eight. Ihya, the last of the daily worship consists of six rak'as worshipped any time between the sunset and evening performances.

Weekly Supererogatory Worship

Considering the excellence of the day of the week, some worships are recommended:-

Yaumul Ahad	Sunday	A 4 rak'a worship after the Salatul Zuhr and another, 20 rak'a worship in the night.
Yaumul Isnain	Monday	2 rak'a worship at the

		advance of Day and 4 rak'a worship in the night.
Yaumul Salasa	Tuesday	10 rak'a worship in the middle of the Day and 2 rak'a worship in the night.
Yaumul Arba	Wednesday	12 rak'a worship at the advance of the Day and 2 rak'a worship in the night.
Yaumul Khanis	Thursday	2 rak'a worship between noon and afternoon and 2 rak'a worship in the night.
Yaumul Juma'h	Friday	2 rak'a worship before congregational worship and 12 rak'a worship between sunset and night worships.
Yaumul Sabt	Saturday	4 rak'a worship in the day time and 12 rak'a worship between sunset and night worships.

Yearly Worship

They consist of four different performance. They are 1. Salatul Idain or the two Worships in connection with Id-al-Fitr (on the first of Shawwal) and Id-al-Adha (tenth of Dul-Hajj). The worships on the Feast days have a high degree of excellence. In fact among the Nafl, Salatul Idain is the most meritorious. Performed in two rak'as preferably on any open ground, the Imam delivers a sermon on the importance of the day. For the worship of al-Fitr, the congregation usually assemble after the alms are distributed, and so the worship takes place at a time almost nearing mid-day. The other worship being held in connection with the Pilgrimage is performed in the morning so that the sacrificial victim can be slaughtered early for distribution of its flesh.

Tarawih (Rest-Giving Worship)

During Ramadan, after the Prescribed Evening Performance, it is enjoined upon the Muslims to pray five Tarawihas of four rak'as each. Thus, they pray 20 rak'as. It is so named because after each Tarawiha, a brief rest is observed, on each rak'a not less than ten Quranic verses are recommended to be recited. Thus about 6,000 are covered in the entire 29 or 30 Tarawih worships (Al-Quran has 6200 verses).

Ramadan is the most excellent month of Islamic Calendar. The fast in Ramadan is believed to burn away the sins of human beings (Rauz). Hence the month is known as Ramadan or Ramazan.

Worship during Rajab (Salat Al-Ragha'ib)

It is a twelve rak'a worship performed on the first Thursday night (Friday night according to Islamic day) of Rajab, the most 'honoured' month of Islamic calendar preceded by a fast for the whole day. Expecting high reward of forgiveness of all sins and the right of intercession for seven hundred relatives, the devout among the Muslims give considerable importance to this worship. Because of the high excellence, it is also known as Salat al-Raghaib.

Worship of Sha'ban (Salat Al-Khair or The Good Worship)

Acclaimed as the lengthiest congregational worship, it consists of a hundred rak'as performed on the eve of the fifteenth of Sha'ban. The reward for each performance is fulfilling seventy needs. Fifteenth Sha'ban is Night of Record. On this Night, it is believed that all actions of mankind for the year will be recorded. So, it is highly meritorious to keep awake the whole night and offer a worship of hundred rak'as.

Occasional Worship

These worships are to be performed on the occurrence of certain events as during eclipses of the Sun and the Moon (Al-Kusuf and Al-Khusuf) and during drought, death etc. Worships of Greetings, Praises, Need and Prosperity and that observed after ablution are also coming under this category of Nafl. In all, there are nine occasional worships. They are mostly of two Rak'as except the worship of Praise (4 Rak'as) worships of al-Kusuf and al-Khusuf are performed in congregation lasting till the eclipses are over. The recommended suras for recital after the Fatiha are the first four long suras. There are two Bowings in each rak'a instead of the usual one. Reciting the sura entitled 'The Cow' (Sura II) in the first Standing of the first rak'a and the Family of Imran (Sura III) in the second Standing after the Bowing (in the first rak'a) and the women (Sura IV) in the third Standing (second rak'a) and the Table (V) in the fourth Standing has excellence. Request for rain after a drought is also performed in groups preceded by a three day fast. It is highly meritorious to give alms liberally to the poor. On the fourth day the people assemble in an open space for the congregational worship. It is recommended to wear old and poor clothes. This two rak'a worship has no Takbir. The Imam addresses the congregation twice with a brief rest between them. In the course of the second Kutba, the Imam turning to the Qibla changes his cloak inside out, making the upside down and right side left. Having the congregation also done this, a supplication is made inaudibly. With the turned cloak on, the congregation disperses.

Worship of the Need

It is an important Nafl Worship performed when a person is in need. It is usually a 12 rak'a worship. Whoever performs a 4 rak'a worship reciting in the first rak'a the Opening Sura and Sura CXII (At-Tauhid) ten times, in the second rak'a Sura I and Sura CXII thirty times and in the last rak'a Sura I and Sura CXII forty times and tnen says the Salutation and recites Sura CXII seventy five times and says the Seeking of Forgiveness of Allah for himself and his parents seventy five times and then makes his request is also a form of worship. But this worship, if over done, defeats the very purpose of worship. For it may lead one to be lazy. Hence, the learned are of the opinion that this form of Worship must not be taught to the unintelligent.

Worship of Greetings to the Mosque

It is a 2 rak'a performance strongly recommended to be performed when one enters or leaves a mosque. It is obligatory even if the Imam is delivering the address. This worship primarily prepares one for the more important Fard worship. A 2-rak'a worship is recommended after the ablution, upon entering and leaving any house. Similarly whenever any one is anxious about a thing, let him perform a two rak'a worship.

Funeral Worship or Salat-Al-Janaza

For the burial of the deal, Islam prescribes many observances and it is made obligatory for every Muslim to make the burial as quickly as possible because if the dead is a virtuous man he would have an early chance of the eternal bliss that would wait upon him.

Having the body of the deceased washed, perfumed cotton is plugged to the orifices of the body and he is wrapped in two white seamless cloth. The burial usually takes places in the morning on the same day and in the morning if the death took place in the late evening or night. Women seldom accompany a funeral. The body is covered in a closed trestle, carried on the shoulders by four persons. The funeral party say the Shahada while they bring the trestle with the body to a mosque for the service prior to burial.

The tomb, which is dug on the ground has an ante-room in the bottom just wide enough to admit the body. It is kept lying on the right side with the head pointing to the Ka'ba. All persons attending the burial are commanded not to depart until the completion of the burial. On entering the burial ground, the funeral party utters words of Peace to the buried. "The peace is upon you, O people of these abodes, of the believers and Muslims, and may Allah have mercy upon those of us who are coming soon, and those who are coming later, for we, if Allah will, are to meet you!" The Salat in connection with the death of a person has the distinction that it has no rak'a. The persons led by the Leader of the Worship say the Takbir four times reciting after the first Takbir the Fatiha, after the second and third, Blessings upon the Prophet and Supplication for the Dead, and then the final Takbir and Salutation.

A last Supplication is said after the dead is buried and the grave is made. "O Allah, Thy Creature has returned to Thee, so have mercy upon him, and show mercy to him! O Allah, remove the earth from his two sides, and open the gates of heaven to his spirit, and receive him unto Thyself with a beautiful welcome, and, if he is a well doer, double for him his good deeds; and, if he is an evil doer, pass by his evil deeds."

A two rak'a Nafl worship is recommended on entering a mosque, after ablution, on entering and leaving a house and on important events as wearing of Ihram and before beginning the Tawaf (Circuit around Ka'ba) and also when requesting for prosperity.

In Islamic worship, ritual purity or Tahara is as important as spiritual purity. Without ritual purity, the worship becomes invalid. Abu Malik has reported that he heard the Messenger of Allah saying that, "purification is half the faith." On another occasion, the Messenger said, "the key to paradise is prayer and the key to prayer is purification." It consists of the cleaning of the body, clothing and place of Worship. "As for the Purification, whenever you purify your place, which is your outermost container, and then your clothing, which is your nearest covering, and then your skin, which is your closed shell, do not be unmindful of your kernel, which is your essence, and that is your heart." Water, which is created pure is the only substance which can be used to remove the impure matter (Najasa) from the body, but water having a change of colour, taste and odour is impure. Otherwise two large jars of water (measuring not less than 266 litres of water) will do for cleansing. Vessels used for this purpose must also be clean. Gold and silver vessels need not be used. In view of the importance of water in Islamic prayer, every mosque has a water tank in its courtyard for the devotees to wash. However, under extreme circumstance of illness or there is difficulty to procure water or if the prayer is late for certain worships, a symbolic method of washing the body with fine soil or sand is recommended. It is called Tayammum

Wuzu

Purification is necessary to remove minor and major impurities. Touching any unclean thing or anything passing out through the bodily orifices cause minor impurities which can be removed by ablution or cleansing of the body (Wuzu). Wuzu, "a means of access, the purpose of which is the worship" is the washing of the hands, arms, ears, face, mouth, feet and rubbing the head with wet hand. It is, in fact, a prefatory and introductory step to worship and is absolutely necessary for the performance of worship. After saying the Niyyat or Intention of Wuzu, he washes his hands, rinses his mouth along with the openings of the nostrils, washes his face from the hairline to the neck and the chin, and then hands up to elbow all three times. (Washing the parts more than three times is blameworthy as it is a wastage of water). Next, he draws his wet right hand over the head, combing the beard with fingers of the right hand. Having this done, he twists his ears with his fore-fingers passing his thumbs at the back of the ears and rubbing from bottom upwards. Lastly, he washes his feet upto the ankles passing his fingers between the toes. After doing all these, he says raising his face towards heaven: "I witness that there is no god but God, the Unique, who has no partner. I witness that Muhammad is His servant and His messenger." Wuzu has four Fard and 14 Sunna regulations. Fard regulations are:

1. Washing the face from the top of the forehead to the chinbetween the ears.
2. Washing the arms up to elbow.
3. Rubbing the head (not less than one fourth) with the wet hand.
4. Washing the feet up to ankles.

Sunna Regulations

1. To make the Intention (Niyyat) of Wuzu (I make this wuzu for the purpose of putting away impurity)
2. To wash the hand up to the wrist.(It is recommended not to put the hands entirely into the water until each hand has been rubbed three times with water poured on it.)
3. To say one of the names of God at the commencement of the ablution.
4. To clean the teeth with Miswak (tooth brush cut out from any tree).
5. To rinse the mouth three times.
6. To put water into the nostrils three times i.e. sriff up water[1]
7. To do all the above in proper order.
8. To do all without any delay between the various acts.
9. Each part is to be purified three times.
10. The space between the fingers of one hand must be rubbed with the wet fingers of the other.
11. The beard must be combed with the wet fingers.
12. The entire head must be rubbed once.
13. The ears must be washed with the water remaining on the fingers after the last operation, and
14. To rub under and between the toes with the little finger of the left hand (between each toe in succession.)

There are seven causes[2] which annul the ablution. They are :

1. If anything comes out of urethra and anus.
2. Loss of consciousness including sound sleep. However light sleep preferably by sitting is excepted.
3. If any repugnant matter comes out through any body openings.
4. Touching the male organ.
5. Touching a woman with desire.
6. Apostacy.
7. Touching impure things such as liquor, pork and dead bodies or animals like dogs, swine etc.

Ghusl

It is the religious washing of every part of the body to remove any legal or major impurity. Ghusl is different from Ghasl which is simply washing. There are four occasions which make the body reli-

---

[1]The Prophet is reported to have sniffed up water with his right hand and blowing up his nose with his left hand.

[2]Some lawyers say eating of camel's flesh annuls the wuzu.

giously impure (Junub). They are

1. Menses (Hayz)
2. Puerperium (Nifas)
3. Coitus (Jima), and
4. Polhitio Nocturna (Ihtilam). In the occurrence of any one or more of them the person is debarred from performing the worship unless he takes Ghusl. As in all Islamic ceremonies Niyyat or Intention is necessary to make Ghusl valid. Having the Niyyat said, he washes his entire body. The sunna of Ghusl is to say, "In the name of God" and rub his body with the hand. Using plenty of water is highly recommended and meritorious.

Tayammum

Tayammum is religious purification by sand or dust instead of water. It is allowed on the following circumstances.

1. If water is not available within a distance of two miles.
2. Being sick, use of water is injurious.
3. To procure water the person has to undergo danger as from enemy, poisonous reptiles or beasts.
4. If the person is late for the Salatul Idain and Salatul Janaza and if the Imam has already started the worship.

The method of performing Tayammum is placing the hands once or more than once on the soil (clean) and rub the face with the hands and then rub the hands together. It should also have the Niyyat and the soil must be pure and dusty.

Clothing

The person must cover the shameful things of the body from the sight of others. The minimum covering is from navel to the knee. Wearing head dress is recommended. The garment one wears at the time of worship must be clean, and free from any legal impurity. If he has doubt about his garment, it is better to wash the entire garment.

Another important feature of Islamic worship is that it is performed facing the Ka'ba in Mecca. One interpretation for facing Ka'ba is to accept God's order to prostrate Adam as angels have prostrated. In the Islamic world, the Ka'ba is the living symbol of the House of God. Facing it, the Muslims all over the world form a circle of Faithful, a circle as wide as the world itself. The Chinese along with the Indians, Malaysians, Persians face west, Ye mens and some Africans face north, the

Russians face, south and the people from Sadan, Niger etc. in Central Africa and Brazilians face east, but all face the Ka'ba. It is their life-goal to visit and pray there. Al-Ka'ba is so sacred a building to the Muslims that they bury their dead, face being placed towards it. All important ceremonies are performed facing Ka'ba.. The direction of the Ka'ba is shown in the mosque with a niche or Mihrab in the centre of the wall where the Imam stands at the time of worships. The salat facing any direction other than the Ka'ba invalidates the worship. Its wilful omission is not permitted except when one is travelling and there is difficulty to locate the direction of the Ka'ba or keep the direction of the Qibla. Or, when one prays in a battle field.

In the early days, Muslims worshipped facing Jerusalem, and while the Prophet was in Medina, he led the prayers facing Jerusalem in the north. However, after eighteen months of his arrival in Medina and in the midst of a congregational worship in a little Mosque in Medina (now known as Jami'al Qiblatayn: The Mosque of two Qiblas) the revelation making the Ka'ba in Mecca the Qibla was received. (Sura II. 144). Without waiting for conclusion of the worship, the Prophet at once turned round to the south towards Mecca. The whole congregation too turned round. Thereafter Mecca, the First City of Islam became the Qibla.

Soon after the fixation of the Ka'ba in Mecca from Jerusalem, the Prophet sought counsel with his companions to adopt a Call to gather the worshippers to the Congregational worship and also announce the hours of Worship. Some suggested bells, others trumpets, but none, probably all suggestions appeared to be imitations, was acceptable. The assembly broke to re-assemble next day. In the night Abdulla ibn Umar had a vision in which a person, presumed to be an angel, clad in green mantle, appeared to him with an instrument in his hand. Abdulla was tempted to buy it to use for gathering the devotees for worship. Thereupon the man in vision had suggested the call. Umar ibn al-Khattab also testified that he had a similar dream. And the Summons or Call to Prayer was accepted. Ever since that day Adhan[1] the passionate call, the most familiar human call emanating from the minarets of a million thousand mosques from all over the Islamic world just before the glorious daybreak and in the stillness of the night has become a special feature of Islamic worship. For the morning worship, when Muadhin

---

[1]Derived from Adhana, meaning to inform. Adhan is giving information at a particular time.

adds, "Prayer is better than sleep!" the hearers will respond, "You have spoken truly. You have given good advice." With the announcement of the Hour of Worship, the world around the mosque suddenly leaps into activity, and the worshippers crowd around the water tanks in the courtyard for the ablution. When the summons for noon and afternoon worships are announced, the pious stop the work whatever the urgency of it, to join the congregation in the mosque. Thus, they go and meet together five times a day, forming a community of Believers. In the courtyard of a mosque, they are humble and pious and they stand shoulder to shoulder in rows and with meticulous unanimity and in humble submission, they stand up to say the Takbir, to recite Al-Fatiha, to bow and prostrate before God. With equal perfection, they conduct the worship to meet again a few hours later.

The MANNER OF WORSHIP

1. Standing Posture (Qiyam)[1]

When he is ready for worship, he stands facing the Qibla and pairs his feet together without joining them. Usually he may not wear shoes, but covering the feet is not prohibited. Facing the Qibla is a stronger preliminary stipulation than the standing Posture, for the latter may be dispensed within the Supererogatory worships or if the Worshipper is ill while the former may be dispensed with only in battle and in parts of a worship performed while travelling and there is difficulty to keep the Qibla. Standing is an indication of reverence and obedience, and so joining up one foot behind the other is a sign of disobedience and is to be avoided. Let his gaze be fixed on the ground or preferably on the spot where his forehead touches in Prostration. It is advisable to mark the limit of the ground. During the worship, the sacred ground should not be traversed by any human being or animal. Keeping the head erect is not desirable, but inclined head is a sign of submission. It also prevents the thoughts wandering away from the theme of worship.

Assuming this posture, he says the four Shurut (Stipulations)[2] of

---

[1]Parts of a worship are many and there is no unanimity by the authors. I have not clearly followed any. In brief there are 4 main postures—Standing, Bowing, Prostration and Sitting.

[2]Singular Shart. Shurut are those upon which the validity of the worship depends. Next in importance is Sunna or Usages. Its omission makes worship valid but incom-

the Worship. (These Stipulations are so important that some commentators consider it as Far'sid (Singular Fard) or Prescribed part of a worship. These are Saying the Formula or Basmalla i.e. "In the name of Allah, the Merciful and Compassionate", and the Tawwudh (Seeking Refuge)

> *"Say: I seek refuge in the Lord of mankind,*
> *the Possessor of mankind,*
> *the God of mankind,*
> *from the evil of the whispers,*
> *the one who goes back,*
> *who whispers in the breasts of mankind,*
> *of the Jinn and mankind."*

Having done this, the Worshipper says the third Shart, that is Adhan of Call to Worshipper (in a Congregational Worship, it is said by the Muadhin).

> *"Allah is great! Allah is great'. (2 times)*
> *I witness, There is no god but Allah! (2 times)*
> *I witness, Muhammad is the Messenger of Allah! (2 times)*
> *Come to worship! (2 times)*
> *Come to prosperity! (2 times)*
> *Allah is great! Allah is great!*
> *I witness, There is no god but Allah."*[1]

It is specially meritorious to respond to the Call of the Muadhin. The devout repeat each sentence of the call with piety. When the Hailatain or Come to Worship! Come to Prosperity! is heard, the hearers say, "There is no might and strength but in Allah!" In the Morning Prayer, Tathwib is added after Hailatain.

"The Worship is better than Sleep!" On hearing this, the followers say, "May Allah institute it and continue it as long as the heavens and the earth continue!" The Worshipper now says:

"O Allah! By the right of this complete call and worship instituted, grant Muhammad meditation and excellence, and elevate him to the praiseworthy station which Thou didst promise him. Thou dost not violate a promise."

---

plete. An omission of Sunna is to be made up by an extra prostration. (Al-Sujud al-Sahu) before the salutation.

[1] Shias say the last phrase twice.

The fourth Shart is Iqamat or Institution which is similar to Adhan with the addition of a sentence that worship is now ready. Having the completion of the fourth shart, the Worshipper is ready to begin the proper worship.

Thus stood erect with solemnity, reverence and humbleness, he says the Niyyat or Intention of the worship that "I perform at its proper time the Prescribed (Noon) Worship to Allah" if it is Noon Worship. (Or Morning, After-noon, Sunset or Night worship as the worship may be) Niyyat is one of the twelve Prescribed Elements of Worship and its omission invalidates the entire worship. Having this done, he raises his hands opposite to his shoulders in such a way that his palms are towards the Qibla and his thumbs opposite to the lobes of his ears and the tips of his fingers opposite the tops of his ears, and when the hands have come for a brief rest in this position, he says the Takbir (Allah Akbar) clearly, forcefully understanding the meaning of each and every word and definitely not carelessly and absent mindedly. This is called Takbir al-Ihram because it is a recitation of the Takbir of Sanctification. When the Takbir is said, he allows the hands to come down as naturally as possible and places the right hand on the left above the navel, below the chest. With the thumb, little[1] and ring fingers of the right hand, he holds the wrist of the left arm. Islam is a religion of marvelous blending of faith, action, and binding. The recital of Takbir (Faith) and the Standing posture and movement of hands (action of obedience and humbleness before God) and placing of hands (binding) are a combined act. That is the Faith that 'God is great' is combined with action (raising of the hands) and binding (holding the left hand with the right hand is a form of binding). Takbir should be said clearly and forcefully. Saying Takbir is the second Prescribed Element. Takbir is the breaking point; the devotee breaks off all connections with earthly matters in order to enter into communion with God. And so it is called Takbir Al-Ihram (Recitation of the Takbir of Sanctification.)

After a brief pause, he says the Introductory Supplication (the Subhan).

> *"Praise is Thine, O Allah!*
> *By Thy praise! Blessed of itself is Thy name,*
> *and exalted is Thy majesty, and sublime is Thy*
> *praise, and there is no god but Thee."*

---

[1]The Schools differ in the manner of placing the hands. The Shafi and Wahabis place their hands on their breasts; the Shias keep their hands on either side.

It is followed by the Tawwudh or Auzubilla : "I seek refuge in Allah from cursed Satan" and Basmalla or Tasmiyah: "In the name of Allah, the Merciful and Compassionate" and Fatiha (Opening Sura).

> *"Praise belongs to Allah, the Lord of the worlds,*
> *the Merciful, the Compassionate, the Ruler of the Day of Judgement.*
> *Thee we worship and Thee we ask for aid*
> *Direct us in the right way, the way of those to whom Thou are gracious not of those Thou art angry with, nor of those who err."*

Recital of Fatiha is the third Prescribed element of Salat and so all the words of the Fatiha must be pronounced clearly and distinctly. It should never be recited in a hurry nor skipped over. If he is not behind an Imam, he may even recite Fatiha audible to hear himself in the Dawn, Sunset and Night Salat. At the end of Fatiha, he says Amin (the Tamin). Next, he recites a Sura or three or more verses of the Quran. Some of the recommended Suras are as follows. For morning worship, any of the lengthy Suras preferably of the Mufassal (the Seven suras beginning from XLIX or the Nine suras from XLV to XCII) is meritorious. For Salat Zuhr, the 85th Sura is excellent. Four short suras are given as specimen:

Sura Kauthar (CVIII)

> *Bismillahir Rahmanir Rahim*
> *Inna a'Tayan Kalkauser Fesalli Lirabbike Venhar Inne Shani' Eke Huvel Ebter.*
> *(In the name of God, the Beneficent, the Merciful)*
> *Lo! We have given thee Abundance: So pray unto thy Lord, and sacrifice*
> *Lo! It is thy insulter (and not thou) who is without posterity.*

Surah At-Tauhid or Ikhlas (CXII)

> *Bismillahir Rahmanir Rahim*
> *Kul Huvallahu Ehad Allahus Samad Lem Yelid Ve Lem Yuled Ve Lem Yekun Lehu Kufuvan Ehad.*
> *(In the name of Allah, the Beneficent, the Merciful)*
> *Say: He is Allah, the One.'*
> *Allah, the eternally Besought of all!*

He begetteth not nor was begotten.
(And there is none comparable unto Him.")

Surah An-Nas (CXIV)

Bismillahir Rahmanir Rahim
Kul Euzu Birabbin Nasi Melikin Nasi Ilahin Nasi Min Sherril Ves Vasil Khannasi
Ellezi Yuvasuvisu Fi Sudurin Nasi Minel Jinneti Vennas."
(In the name of Allah, the Beneficent, the merciful,
Say; I seek refuge in the Lord of mankind,
The king of mankind,
The God of mankind,
From the evil of the sneaking whisper,
Who whispereth in the hearts of mankind,
Of the jinn and of mankind.")

Surah Al-Falaq (CXIII)

Bismillahir Rahmanir Rahim
Kul Euzu Birabbi Felaki Min Sherri Ma Khalaka Ve Min Sherri Gaskin Iza Vekaba
Ve Min Sherrin Neffasati Fil Ukadi Ve Min Sherrin Hasidin Iza Hasad."
(In the name of Allah, the Beneficent, the Merciful
Say; I seek refuge in the Lord of Daybreak
From the evil of that which He created;
From the evil of the darkness when it is intense.
And from the evil of malignant witchcraft
And from the evil of the environment when he envieth.")

After this, the worshipper is ready for the second posture, that is Bowing (Rukku). Raising both hands, he says Takbir and bends down, placing the palms of his hands on his knees, separating the fingers little. Rukku is the fourth Prescribed Element of worship. In this position, back, neck and head should be in line. (But a woman may keep her elbow at her sides). In Rukku he says not less than three times "Subhane Rabbiyee Azim" ("I extol the holiness of my Lord, the Great")[1]- Then slowly he comes up to the Standing Posture, raises his hands as before for the Takbir and says "Semi Allahu Limen Hamide Rabbena

---

[1]Shias say "I extol the holiness of my Lord, the Great and with His Praise."

Lekal Hamd" (Allah hears whoever says His praise' O Lord, Thou art praised.") This is Tasmi. In the morning worship after Tasmi, he recites Qunut in the second Rak'a with both hands raised towards heaven kept almost parallel to the face.[1] The Qunut is recited as follows:

"O God, we seek help from Thee, and forgiveness of sins
We believe in Thee and trust in Thee
We praise Thee. We thank thee. We are not unthankful
We expel, and we depart from him who does not obey Thee
We serve Thee only, and to Thee do we pray
We seek Thee, we prostrate ourselves and we serve Thee
We hope for Thy mercy. We fear Thy punishments
Surely Thy Judgements are upon the infidels."

Straightening from the position of bowing and standing for a brief moment is the sixth Prescribed Element.

II. PROSTRATION (TASBIH-I-SIJDAH)

Next he goes down for the Prostration saying the Takbir. In the Prostration he places the knees on the ground followed by hands, forehead and nose. In this posture, his elbow must be away from the side (women exempted). Care is to be taken not to separate the finger but they should be kept joined as naturally as possible. Having thus prostrated, he recites thrice Tasbih "Sub' hane Rabbiyel A'ala" ("I extol the holiness of my Lord, the Most High"). Saying Tasllih more than three times is meritorious. Rising from the Prostration, he says the Takbir and sits on his right foot and places his hands on his thighs with the fingers extended. Prostration and Straightening from it are the two Prescribed Elements. In this position, he says,"O Lord, forgive me! Have mercy on me! Provide for me! Guide me! Preserve me in health and pardon me.' "[2] Immediately he goes down for the second Prostration and recital as before. Then he rises up saying the Takbir as before. Then he rises up saying the Takbir for Standing Posture keeping not his legs forward but by placing his hands on the ground. This complete the first Rak'a or Cycle of performance.

---

[1]There is a strong Tradition for this, Raising hands in Qunut is a fitting supplication and is preferred.

[2]The Shias say, "I rise and sit by the power of God! God is great."

The Witnessing

In the second Rak'a after the Second Prostration is over, he rises his head and sits on his left leg placing his right hand on his right thigh, folding his right fingers except the index finger which he points when he recites 'Allah' and not when he recites, 'There is no god'[1]

First Witnessing or Tahiyah

Ettehiyatu Lillahi Vesselavatu
Vettayyibatu Esselamu Aleyke
Eyyuhennebiyyu Ve Rahmetullahi Ve
Berekatuhu Esselamu Aleyna Ve Ala
Ibadillahssalihin.

"The greetings belong to Allah! Peace be upon thee, O Prophet,
And the mercy and blessing of Allah!
Peace be upon us,
And upon the righteous creatures of Allah! "Then he says the Tashaud as follows:

"Eshhedu En Lailahe Illallah Ve Eshhedu Enne Muhammeden Abduhu Ve Rusuluh"

("I witness: There is no god but Allah! and Muhammad is the Messenger of Allah!")
When he say "but Allah!" he opens the first finger of the right hand.

It is followed by Blessing upon the messenger and the family (Darud).

"Allahumme Salli ala Muhammedin Ve ala ali Muhammadin Kema Salleyte ala-Ibrahime Ve ala ali Ibrahim inneke hamidun Majid.
Allahumme Barik ala Muhammadin Ve ala ali Muhammadin Kema Barkte Ala Ibrahime Ve ala ali Ibrahim inneke Hamidum Mejid."

("O Allah! Bless the Messenger of Allah, and on his descendants as Thou didst have mercy on Abraham and on his descendants. Thou art to be praised, and Thou art great. O God, bless Muhammad and his descendants as Thou didst bless Abraham and his descendants praised, and Thou art great!")

Next is Du'a. "Rubbena Atina Fiddunya Haseneten Ve Fil Akhireti Haseneten Ve Kina Ozabennar." (''O God our Lord give us the bles-

---

[1] Shias omit this.

sings of this life, and also the blessings of life everlasting. Save us from the torments of fire.")

Sitting for the Last Witnessing and Saying the Last Witnessing are the tenth and eleventh Prescribed Elements. In the Last Witnessing that is second Rak'a of the morning, fourth Rak'a of noon, evening and night worships, and third Rak'a of sunset worship, he sits by placing left foot extends out from under him towards the right. Then he says, Esselamu Aleykum Ve Rahmetullahu" ("The Peace is upon you, and the mercy of Allah") and he turns to the right so that his right cheek may be seen from behind on the right side. This is the twelfth prescribed Element. Similarly, he turns to the left and gives the Salutation. This is called Taslim-Al-Tahlil because it is the Salutation of the desanctification, sanctification began with the first Takbir. For leaving off the worship also, he must have the Intention.

After each worship it is meritorious to recite Ayetul Kursi followed by reciting 33 times each "Subhanalla" ,"Elhamdu lillah" and "Allahu Akbar." There are twelve Prescribed Elements in Worship. Omission of even one of the following Prescribed Elements invalidates the entire worship.

1. The Intention
2. The Takbir
3. The Standing Posture
4. Saying the Fatiha
5. Bending down in the Bowing until the palms reach the knees with coming rest in it.
6. Straightening from the Bowing and Standing up.
7. Prostration excluding the placing of the hands.
8. Rising from this position and sitting.
9. The sitting for the Last Witnessing.
10. The Last Witnessing.
11. The Blessing upon the Prophet, and
12. The First Salutation.

The following are the twelve Sunna or Usages connected with the Invocation

1. The Introductory Supplication.
2. The Seeking Refuge.
3. Saying 'Amin' after Fatiha.
4. Reciting a Sura from the Quran.
5. The Takbir of the transitions, that is, the change of positions

between the Standing, Bowing, Prostration and Sitting Postures.
6. Invocation in the Bowing.
7. Invocation in the Prostration.
8. Straightening from Bowing and Prostration.
9. The First Witnessing.
10. Blessing upon the Prophet.
11. Supplication at the end of the Last Witnessing.
12. The Second Salutation.

SOME IMPORTANT RULINGS

Worship is communion with God, and absolute silence is to be observed throughout. Unnecessary body movements are not tolerated. If any flea, mite or louse disturbs the worshipper and he suffers on account of it or if he apprehends any attack or bite from any poisonous animal or reptile as from scorpion and if he is distracted by it from the worship, he may get rid of it by brushing it away or by killing it with not more than two blows or scratches, for three blows make too many and invalidates the worship. Similarly, in a worship only three slight motions from correct postures are allowed. However, placing the hand on the mouth at the time of yawning is permitted. Similarly, saying " O Praise to Allah!" is also allowed but it should be inaudible without any tongue movement. Rearranging the dress in the course of worship is disliked, but it may be done if falling away of dress oppresses the worshipper or if he is in discomfort. Worshipping wearing footwears is not disallowed. Coughing and expectoration are eventhough disliked do not make the worship invalid. A tradition states that the Prophet has permitted a person to expectorate on the loose ends of his cloak than spitting on the floor or wall of the place of worship. Further, it is related that the Prophet was annoyed when he saw phlegm on the wall of the mosque. He scratched it away from the wall with a stick and applied scent over it.

Worship with no head-cover is condemned in Islam. If it is out of laziness it amounts to Makruh (Abominable)."The Turban," said the Prophet," is a frontier between Faith and unbelief." Head-dress and cap are so important for a Muslim, he never appeared on important occasions with his head open. Standing alone in a row in a congregational worship is disliked, but does not make it invalid. To avoid this, it is better if he enters into a row or draw one from the row himself.

FRIDAY CONGREGATIONAL WORSHIP (SALAT AL-JUMA)

Friday is a great day for Muslims. Definitely it is not a day of rest, as Sunday is to a Christian, but on that day the Muslims are commanded to participate in Congregational worship and having finished, to continue their avocation. Many are the Prophetic sayings on the excellence of Friday. "On Friday Adam was formed. On it he was introduced into the Garden and on it he was cast down to the earth, on it he was forgiven and on a Friday he died; on it the Resurrection Hour will come, and is, with Allah, the day of increase! So the angels name it in heaven, and it is the day for seeing Allah, in the Garden." It is so sacred a day, "whoever dies on Friday, or on the eve of Friday, has Allah decree for him the reward of a martyr and preservation from the testing of the grave.[11] In another saying, ''it is given, if Friday is safe all days are safe.''

The congregational Worship, popularly known as Salat al-Juma is obligatory for all male Muslims who attained puberty and are sane and residing in a village or township where at least forty Muslims reside. Eligible means forty male free Muslims who are mature and sane. A village for this purpose comprises all the houses which can hear the Adhan when the Muadhin gives the Call to prayer in a good voice. On hearing the Call, all activities cease and the people assemble in the chief mosque (Jama Masjid) for worship. Juma worship is compulsory for all and exceptions from participation in the congregation are given only on genuine grounds. The attendant of a sick man, if he is the only attendant can secure an exemption from Friday Congregational Worship. On account of fear, heavy rain or illness, one may instead of the Juma Worship, make an ordinary four Rak'a Noon worship.

It is highly meritorious if the preparation for the Juma worship begins from at least one day preceding the worship that is on the eve of Thursday after the Asr prayer. Washing the clothes is favoured. Fasting on Friday is also meritorious and recommended. Reading Quran on Thursday night has special reward. It is obligatory for all the participants to take a bath. Persons attending the mosque without taking bath are disliked. Before pouring water over his body let him say the Niyyat or the Intention that he bathes for the Friday observance. However, if he suffers from legal impurity and to be free from it, he has to say the Niyyat a second time or let him have a combined Niyyat for the removel of legal impurity and observance of Juma Worship. Appearing in the mosque in shabby clothes is as far as possible to be avoided. On the contrary, a person coming to a mosque clean is appreciated and even rewarded. Let him shave the hair, pare the nails, trim the moustache and perfume the body. The Prophet paid utmost attention to cleanliness. He was a model unto himself. For Friday Services, he used to cleanse his clothes and bathe himself. Without being assisted by anybody, he used to go alone to the mosque to lead the Friday Prayer. On arriving there he would greet the people first without waiting for them to greet him, and then he would ascend the pulpit. Having this done, he would again wish the people before sitting down.

Wearing white garments is preferred and even recommended but not compulsory. However wearing black garments or clothes having stains or distinct marks in it is advised to be avoided as far as possible. Wearing a head-dress on Friday is meritorious but he may remove it before or after the worship if it oppresses him because of excessive heat. But when he is coming to the mosque or at the time of worship or when the Imam delivers the sermon, covering the head is preferred. Reaching the mosque early carries special reward.

Detailed instructions are given to the devotee. He must enter the mosque politely without oppressing any one who is already sitting there. The new entrant is restricted in passing over the necks of the people or pass before them. Standing close to the Imam has a reward. On account of this speical merit, elderly people always seek the first row. When the Imam ascends to the minbar for delivering the Khutba, the congregation must stop offering preliminary worships so that they can closely attend the sermon.

Khutba or Sermon in Juma worship is very important, and hearing it has special merit. The Khutba is said by Khatib. The Khutba consists of an eulogy (Khutbat Al-Nat) and a pious Exhortation (Khutbat Al-Waz). In the Khutbat Al-Nat the Preacher usually prays for blessings on the ruler. The Imam, when the Muadhin has proclaimed the Adhan, stands up on the second step of the pulpit (Minbar)[1] and delivers the oration in Arabic. It has two sections and in between them, the Imam makes a supplication by sitting. It is also recorded that the Prophet used

---

[1] Minbar is a wooden device with three steps kept at the right side of the Mihrab or direction showing the Ka'ba. In the time of the Prophet, he used to address from the third step.

to deliver the sermon from the third step of the Pulpit in such a way that 'his eyes used to be red and his voice high, and his anger raged.' In the way of example, he used to show or raise his finger. To impress upon his audience of the nearness of Resurrection, he showed his fore-finger and the middle finger and said, "Resurrection is as near as these two fingers." i.e. very near. It can be expected any moment, any day.

Remaining in the mosque, after the worship is over for performing Asr and if possible for Sunset worship is excellent.

Special Friday Worship has six additional Stipulations.

1. Time

Time is an important factor for all worships in Islam, and observance of them in their proper hours has special merit. However, doing them in the begining of the time is meritorious. Congregational worships are always held in the beginning of the fixed time. If the salutation of the Imam occurs within the time of Asr, the time for Friday Worship is over.

2. Locality

Juma Worship is observed by not less than forty matured, sane, male Muslims in any immovable buildings and not in any temporary building, tent or open space or plains.

3. Number

From the beginning to the end, the congregation must contain not less than forty Muslim males who are free, responsible, and domiciled (in the same village, town or locality). Domiciled means those who do not move away out of the locality on seasons (winter or summer). If any time the number becomes less than forty, during or before the worship, that worship becomes invalid.

4. Congregation

Holding the worship in different parties by forty or more people of a village makes it invalid. However, if a person is late to join the congregation and if he missed the first Rak'a, he may join the congregation for the one rak'a and himself doing the second rak'a alone. If he joins the congregation after the bowing of the Imam for second rak'a the late comer may follow the Imam and finish it as the regular Noon Worship.

5. Holding more than one Friday Worship by the people of a village

without genuine, valid and fair reasons makes the worship invalid. However, holding more than one congregation is permissible for want of space in the chief mosque.

6. The two addresses are Prescribed, and Standing up during the addresses and Sitting down between them are also Prescribed. Hearing both the addresses is obligatory.

DUTIES OF IMAM

Islam does not recognise priesthood. Nor it approves sainthood. With the elimination of all intermediaries, the Worship in Islam is a direct approach to God. A Muslim may enter into a worship at any place he likes. But if there are three Muslims, one of the them must lead the others. Imam is a leader, simple and pure who leads the people in worship. It is not an office. Worship beheind every faithful man, be he of good or bad behaviour is valid.[1] The Imam is prohibited from accepting any reward for the leadership, for a prophetic saying clearly restraining him. It says, "worship is better when a reward is not accepted for it."[2]

Imam has duties before and after the worship, during the Recital and in the Elements of Worship. There are six duties before the worship, three each during the Recital, in the Elements and after the Worship.

A. Duties before the Worship

1. The Imam must be a learned man and one liked by at least the majority of the people assembled for worship. It is obviously disliked and discouraged to lead the worship by a less learned when there is a more learned man in the Congregation. However, if the latter refuses the leadership there is no objection for him to lead the worship.

2. The Imam is a leader and is recommended not to combine the leadership with the duties of a Muadhin. The Prophetic saying is that the leadership is more excellent than the office of Muadhin. Only the learned among the congregation is permitted to lead the worship. And one having

---

[1]Article 13. The Faith Akbar II. The Muslim Creed, A. J. Wensinck. p. 192

[2]Even taking something for sustenance from the mosque or individual or the ruler is disliked, but not unlawful.

a sonorous voice acts as Muadhin. During the time of the Prophet, he took the leadership of congregational worship and Bilal announced the Adhan. In the absence of the Prophet, Abu Bakr and Umar led the worship.

3. Performing the congregation in the beginning of the appointed time is meritorious and hence the Imam must not wait for anybody. It is said that once Abdul Rahman ibn Auf did not wait for the Prophet who was a bit late (to the extent of time required for ablution) for a Pre-dawn worship. When it was over, the Prophet remarked" You did well in doing that and keep on doing so."[1] However Muadhin must wait only for Imam for giving Institution of the Worship.

4. The Imam must be conscious of the purification and the stipulation of the worship. Without accepting any reward, he must lead the congregation. Worship is better if it is performed without any reward (in money or kind) paid. In fact the reward for worship is incalculable and it cannot be paid in cash. He must be aware of the impurities that debar him from offering worship. Per chance he discovers legal impurity on the person or he recalls any uncleanliness, let him appoint another Imam by taking hand of the one who is near him.

5. The Imam as leader must say the first Takbir only when the people behind him are ready. That is he has to wait till they stand in rows. To make sure that they are ready, let him turn to the right and then to the left. Similarly, before saying the Takbir he has to wait till the Muadhin finishes the Institution for the worship.

6. Let him make sure that the Institution of leadership is made. The Takbirs are always said audibly (but not the followers).

B. During the Recital

1. The Opening Supplication and the Seeking Refuge are to be recited inaudibly while the recital of Fatiha and the accompanying Sura (in the 2 Rak'a of Dawn, Evening and Sunset) is to be made audible. The Amin after Fatiha is said all together, both Imam and the followers (Imam Shafi is of opinion that even Basmallah must also be said aloud.)

2. Waiting for three pauses in Standing Posture, first and the longest after the Takbir enabling the followers to recite Fatiha while the Imam is reciting the Opening Supplication, the second pause is after he had finished Fatiha enabling those who failed to recite it in the first pause

[3]Worship in Islam. pp. 134-5

to finish it, and the third is a brief pause after finishing the sura and before he bows.

3. To recite two suras from the Mathani in the Morning worship. However, finishing the worship before daybreak is preferred. The recital of part of a sura is disputed by the learned. But the Prophet used to recite part of Sura Yunus (x). It is also related that in a Morning Worship, he recited one verse from Sura COW (II) verse 136 (We believe in Allah _ _ _ _ _ _ _ _ _ _resigned) and in the second Rak'a verse 53, Sura III (Our Lord! we believe in that _ _ _ _ _ _ _ _ _ _ _ _ _ written). For Noon Worship upto 30 verses and in the Afternoon worship about 15 verses of Mufassal is recommended. The Prophet, so goes a Tradition, has recited the Sura The Sent One (LXXVII) in his last worship.

C. In the Prescribed Elements

1. Not prolonging the Bowing and Prostration. Eventhough the Saying the Praise ten times is meritorious in single prayers, saying it three times in congregation is preferred. In other words, the congregational worship must be brief and quick and prolonging it by reciting long suras and saying praises more than the required number is not desired.

2. The Imam must bow and prostrate first, and not in unison with the congregation. The followers must bend for prostration not before the forehead of the Imam touches the ground. Similarly, they bend for Bowing not before the Imam completes the Bowing.

3. The Supplication of the Witnessing should not be long and should be for the entire people. Say 'We' and not 'I'.

D. Finishing of the Worship

1. Have the Intention of Salutation upon the people and the angels.

2. Remain stationary for a little while after the Salutation, and perform the supererogatory worship preferably in another place.

3. Having finished, let him turn his face towards the congregation and it is desirable for the people to sit till the Imam turns to them. He must also be aware not to turn back before the women Prayers left the congregation.

WORSHIPS OF THE TWO FEASTS (IDD-AL-FITAR AND IDD-AL-ADHA)

All the festivals in Islam are accompanied by supererogatory worships of which the Salatal Idain, observed in connection with the festivals of Id al Fitr and Id al Adha, are important. Festival worships differ from ordinary worships. The following are the seven prescribed elements for Festival worships.

1. To say the Takbir in series of three utterances as follows. "Allah is great! Allah is great! Allah is great! (first series) Much praise belongs to Allah. (second series)
Praise belongs to Allah morning and evening! There is no god but Allah only!
He has no associate! We devote to Him our religion sincerely even though the unbelievers disapprove!" (third series)

2. The devotees take bath, wear good clothes (silk clothes forbidden) and perfume the body. Cloak and turban are recommended for men.

3. In keeping with a Tradition of the Prophet, it is considered meritorious to take different roads while going for the worship and returning homes. Reciting Takbir on the way to the place of worship has reward.

4. It is preferred to hold the congregation in an open space except in Mecca and Jerusalem or if there is rain.

5. To perform the worship in time. The prescribed hour is between the rising of the sun and its passing the meridian. In order to quicken the slaughtering of animals, it is preferred to perform the worship of Adha'' early. Similarly, as the worship of Fitr is observed after the distribution of alms, its performance is delayed.

6. The Imam who leads the worship need not observe any additional Nafl worship and immediatlely on his arrival he leads the congregation to worship. While Standing he says the opening Takbir and then, he repeates it seven times. In between two Takbirs, he says, "O the Praise of Allah! The Praise belongs to Allah! There is no god but Allah! Allah is greater! I have turned my face toward Him who originally divided the heavens and the earth." After he had said the eighth Takbir, he recites the Seeking of Refuge and then Fatiha, and after Fatiha, Surat Qaf (L). Including the usual two Takbirs for Standing and Bowing, he recites seven Takbir in the second Rak'a, at the same time saying in between two Takbir as for the first Rak'a. In the end he sits down and says the two addresses.

7. He sacrifices a sheep. It is preferred if he himself slaughter the victim by saying,"In the name of Allah! and Allah is greater." There is no objection if he eats the flesh of the sacrificial animal.

Excluding the occasional worships performed on the occurrence of events like eclipse, drought and worship of the need, prosperity, praise etc. a devout Muslim has to pray not less than four hundred and fifty four Rak'as (less 2 if he performs the Friday Juma worship instead of the usual noon worship on Friday) on every week. The following table gives the number of daily worships commanded to be observed with the number of Rak'as.

Day of the week	Fard	Daily Nafl	Weekly Daytime	Night time	Total
SUNDAY	17	35	4	20	76
MONDAY	17	35	2	4	58
TUESDAY	17	35	10	2	64
WEDNESDAY	17	35	12	2	66
THURSDAY	17	35	2	2	56
FRIDAY	17*	35	2	12	66*
SATURDAY	17	35	4	12	68
TOTAL	119*	245	36	54	454*

If the number of Rak'as of all the yearly worships performed by the most pious are added to this, the number comes to unbelievably great for during the full month of Ramadan one prays about 600 Rak'as of Tarawih at the rate of 20 Rak'as of worship each night. Similarly, Nafl worship of Sha'ban has 100 Rak'as. After every ablution two rak'as of Nafl worships is also commanded to be performed.

In actual hours, a pious Muslim must reserve 8.21 per cent of his time[1] for worship alone—both compulsory and supererogatory. So great was the time required, it is no wonder that too many Muslims won't get this much time for all these devotional exercises. It is far from their fault; the world is changed so much. In the present set up, the main occupation robs them most of their time. Moreover, the frequency of ritual worship of 5 times a day, cannot keep pace with our fast modern life. If all the daily supererogatory worships are added to

*If he performs the Juma Worship, it is less by two Rak'as.

[1] Calculated on the basis of the actual time prayed by the author's wife.

this, the number of worships a devout Muslim must pray becomes unimaginably great. It is oppressive to a common man who despite his great urge to pray, finds it impracticable without sacrificing some.of his privations. However there are many faithful performers of the daily compulsory liturgical worships who pray five times every day and attend to their normal duties in office and in their private life and lead a better life than many of us.

With the conclusion of the consideration of Salat as the most important form of prayer, we will pass on to a brief consideration of other forms of prayer enjoined on the Muslims. Next in importance is Al-Tilawa. Imam Ghazali in his book Ihya considers Al-Tilawa or Solemn and pious recital of Al-Quran as a form of prayer. Al-Quran is very syllable divine and its recital is meritorious. By constant training there are devotees who could complete reading the entire Book of 114 chapters (some 6239 verses) in a day and night. Some others can read it from cover to cover twice in a day. Taking ablution (Wudu) and making the surrounding clean before the solemn recital are the recommended acts. Reading aloud so as to hear himself is the best form of Tilawa. The recital should also be clear and forceful.

Invocation (Dhikr) or constant remembrance of God by repeatedly saying the names of Allah is the next recommended duty. God has ninety-nine beautiful names. All these names or a few selected names are used for invocation besides saying Al-Tahlil that is ('There is no god but Allah'), al-Tasbih (the Praise of Allah) and Al-Tahmid ("The Praise or thanks giving belongs to Allah.")

The last act of prayer is Du'a or Supplication made for needs. Du'a also includes the supplication made for God's Forgiveness and Blessings upon the Prophet. The preferred occasions for Supplication are;

1. On the day of Arafa during the Pilgrimage on Dul-Haj;
2. In the month of Ramadan;
3. On every Friday;,
4. After the Fard Worships;
5. On fast days;
6. When facing the Qibla,
7. Repeating the request thrice on being repentent towards Allah.

Al-Wird

It is the manner of spending certain periods in Invocation, Supplication, Recital of the Quran and meditation. The best wird or preiods

FARD WORSHIP		NAFL (SUPEREROGATORY) WORSHIP									
		DAILY		WEEKLY				YEARLY			
				1. DAYTIME		2. NIGHT TIME		1. FIXED FOR OCCASION		2. ON EVENTS	
NAME	NO. OF RAK'AS	NAME	NO. OF RAK'AS	NAME	NO. OF RAK'AS	NAME	NO. OF RAK'AS	NAME	NO. OF RAK'AS	NAME	NO. OF RAK'AS
DAWN	2	Dawn (before Fard)	2	Sunday before Fard)	4	Eve of Sunday (after-noon worship)	20	Id al Fitr Id al Adha	2	Eclipse of sun Eclipse of moon	2
NOON	4	Noon (before Fard) (after Fard)	4 4	Monday (advance of the day)	2	Eve of Monday	4	Tarawih 20 Rak'a per worship	600	Request for rain Salat after wudu	2^{+} 2^{+}
AFTER-NOON	4	After-noon (before (before Fard)	4	Tuesday (middle of the day)	10	Eve of Tuesday	2	Salat of Rajab	12	Greeting of Mosque	2^{+}
SUNSET	3	Sunset (after Fard)	2	Wednesday (advance of the day)	12	Eve of Wednesday	2	Salat of Sha'ban	100	Worship of entering and leaving a house	2^{+}
NIGHT	4	Night (after Fard)	4	Thursday (between Noon and after-noon)	2	Eve of Thursday	2			Worship for prosperity	2^{+}
		Witr	3^{+}	Friday (before Juma)	2	Friday (between sunset and evening	12			Worship of Praise	4^{+}
		Duha (after-noon)	8^{+}	Saturday	4	Saturday (between sunset and evening)	12			Worship of Need	12^{+}
		Enlivening	6								
TOTAL	17		35^{+}		36		54		716		30^{+}

+ No fixed number

for this form of prayer in the Day are between Dawn and Sunruse, between Sunrise and noon, noon and mid-after noon, mid afternoon and sunset. In the night there are five Wirds—two before sleep and one during the sleeping time and two after sleeping time.

ITIKAF

Spending the time of two worships in a mosque for performing as much Nafl worship is Itikaf. The preferred days are Fridays and the last days of Ramadan. Birthday of the Prophet (Mawlid) is celebrated for offering special petition. Visit to tombs (Ziyara) to offer worship is the last form of devotional exercise. But the Wahabhis[1] strongly condemn Ziyara.

THIRD PILLAR OF ISLAM

Zakat or Alm-giving

Zakat or Legal alms, literally purification is the third religious duty prescribed for the votaries of Islam. Man, as a gregarious animal has a bounden duty to the members of the society, and Islam, well deserving to its preachings had made payment of charity or Poor rate compulsory to its followers especially to the rich to strengthen the weaklings of the community. They are so faithful in helping the poor and needy brethren, the debtors and the travellers that in all Islamic countries, there are state appointed Muqaddis to collect the statutary alms and organise its correct distribution. Besides Zakat, Islam also encourages voluntary alms i.e., Sadaqah (pl. Sadaqat), which manifests righteousness. Alms is everything in Islam. Caliph Omar used to say,"Prayer carries us half-way to God, Fasting brings us to the door of His palace, and Alms procure us admission."[2] Alms begin from one's service to himself, to his kith and kin, and to the people at large. In this wider sense, a smile, a good word even to the extent of clearing off the pathways of its nuisance are alms and if performed are rewarded. Richly deserving to the importance of Idul-Fitr, Islam also enjoins its followers to distribute half a Sa' of wheat or flour or fruit and one Sa' of barley before the Festival Prayer. It has become almost compulsory that every rich Muslim gives in alms much more than the prescribed quantity before they set out for the Festival Prayer.

---

[1] One of the several sects of Islam. Its founder is Abdul Wahab.

[2] An History of Mussalman. p. 292. Charles Mills

Islam forbids amassing wealth in any form without utilising at least a portion of it for the common good. Cheerful givers of well gotten wealth are highly praised and promised double repayment. Al-Quran Sura II(Cow) is explicit about it. It says: "Believers, bestow in alms a part of what We have given you before that day arrives when there shall be neither trading nor friendship nor intercession."

Again, "Believers, give in alms of the wealth you have lawfully earned and of that which We have brought out of the earth for you, not worthless things which you yourselves would only reluctantly accept." What can be given in alms. "What ye have to spare" is the Quranic answer (Sura II). On the contrary who hoard treasures and employ it not for the cause of true religion, will receive a severe punishment. Their hoards will be heated in the fire of hell and they will be stigmatised with it on their forelocks, backs and sides. (Sura IX. Repentance).

Zakat differs from Sadaqah as its payment is compulsory to all the categories of persons who have properties or income beyond the prescribed limit for personal use. On the contrary, for the payment of Sadaqah, there is no compulsion which one may give of his own free will. Together with Sadaqah, Zakat form one of the basic foundations of Islam. If properly collected and distributed, it redeems the society of its major deficiency, that is inequality.

Alms must be given with good intention for the sake of God. Those who give alms with taunts, mischief and show are compared in the Quran to a rock covered with sand. When rain falls, the earth is washed away exposing the hardened rock. On the contrary, alms given for the love of God is like a garden. With every shower of rain, it yields more. "What is better than alms followed by mischief?" asks the Sacred Text. "A fair speech, and forgiveness is better than alms followed by insult" (Sura II). Again it says," If ye make your alms to appear, it is well; but if ye conceal them, and give them unto the poor, this will be better for you, and will atone for your sins." (Sura II. 77). Givers of alms are highly praised by the Prophet who was an example unto himself. From his death-bed, he had asked his wife to give away in charity a few coins he had in his house. In the Book of Tradition, it is said: "Your smiling in your brother's face is alms, and your exhorting mankind to virtuous deeds is alms and your showing men the road when they lose it is alms, and your assisting the blind is alms, and your pouring water from your bucket into that of your brother is alms for you."

Quran is explicit on alms-giving. It is so important a duty to the Muslims, Prayer and Alms-giving together is mentioned in al-Quran 24 times, besides almsgiving alone occurs 23 times. This brings out the prominence of almsgiving. It is second only to Salat for its importance. If Salat is for self purification, almsgiving reminds one of his responsibility to create a healthy society where no weaklings crave for food. Prophet is said to have declared that "whosoever refuse to pay the legal alms shall have a serpent twisted round his neck at the resurrection." (Sura III)

Zakat is to be paid for all properties owned and possessed by an adult, sane Muslim for at least one year (if possession is for less than one year, Zakat need not to be paid, but on the twelfth month, it is due) but upon the necessaries of life, slaves employed in service, books, craftmen's tools, and similar other essential tools and commodities required for ones own personal use no Zakat is to be paid. Eventhough prescribed injunctions are available for the quantum of alms to be given for certain commodities, on the basis of the precepts of the Sacred Text, and the Sunna, Charity is compulsory for all possessions, owned for twelve months. Exempted are those things meant for ones personal use such as clothing, furniture etc. or the cattle or other animals employed in tilling the soil or used for carrying burdens. The debtors, who own property but have debts equal to or more than its value are also exempted from Zakat. On the contrary, such debtors are eligible to receive alms. Usually Zakat is one in forty or $2^{1}/_{2}\%$ of the value. The following detailed prescriptions occur in Fiqh.

I. Agricultural Produce

Zakat is due for corn, fruits and for all other agricultural produce. If the cultivation is carried out without irrigation i.e., depending on natural water namely, rivers, rain etc. Zakat is one-tenth of the annual harvest. It is one-twentieth of the annual harvest, if the land is irrigated, water being obtained by any means of machinery, buckets or with the help of animals. Exempted are minor products like grass, bamboo and wood.

II. Animals

Keepers of animals, stall-fed or kept on pasture for the greater part of the year and not fed in the home with forage must give Zakat on the following shares of their possessions.

(a) Camels

Upto	4	camels	No Zakat as it is the minimum required for one's personal use.
5	to	9	1 goat / Sheep
10	to	19	2 goats / Sheep
20	to	24	3 goats/Sheep
25	to	35	1 one-year old female camel (Bint Mikhaz)
36	to	45	1 two-year old female camel (Bint Labun)
46	to	60	1 three-year old female camel (Hiqqa
61	to	74	1 four-year old female camel (Jazah)
75	to	90	2 two-year old female camel (Jazah)
91	to	120	2 three-year colts
121	or	more	calculated on the aforesaid rule

(b) Cows, Bulls and Buffaloes

Upto 29	No Zakat
30 to 39	1 one-year calf (Tabiah)
on reaching 40	1 two-year calf (Musim)
41 or above	On the above proportion. i.e.
Upon 60	2 yearling calves
Upon 70	1 Tabiah + 1 Musim
Upon 80	2 Musims
Upon 90	3 Tabiah
Upon 100	2 Tabiah and 1 Musim

Every 10 above 100, a Musim or Tabiah alternatively. i.e.

110	2 Musims + 1 Tabiah
120	4 Tabiah

The normal practice is to divide by 30 or by 40 and for each 30, one Tabiah and for each 40, one Musim)

(c) Sheep and Goat

They are taken together for the purpose of Zakat. Ghanam is the word used in Tradition which is either sheep or goat or both.

Upto 39	No Zakat
40 to 120	1 goat/Sheep
121 to 200	2 goats/Sheep
201 or above	2 goats/Sheep + 1 goat/Sheep for every 100 in possession.

(d) Horses and Mares

Only the horses and mares meant for merchandise are taken together into consideration for Legal alms. The prescribed rate is one Dinar per head or 5% of the total value which excludes all beasts of burden and animals kept for ploughing etc.

III. Gold and Silver

The proportion of Zakat for possession of metals viz. Gold and Silver is calculated on the following basis. Zakat is due for the metals in any form whether it is manufactured or bullion or ornaments. If it is an alloy for the purpose of charity, the entire value is considered and not the silver or gold contents of it alone.

Gold		*Silver*	
Zakat is one-fortieth of the whole.		Upto 199 Dirhams	No Zakat
		200 - 239 Dirhams	5 Dirhams
Upto 19 Misqals	No Zakat	240 - (Upon reaching)	1 Dirham Extra (6 Dirhams)
20 Misqals	1/2 a Misqal		
Above 20 misqal @ 2 Kirat		Above 240 Dirhams for every succeeding 40 extra	1Dirham
		i.e. for 280	6+1=7 Dirhams
		320 Dirhams	6+1+1=8 Dirhams
		360 Dirhams	6+1+1+1=9 Dirhams

IV. Merchandise

2½% upon the value if it exceeds 200 Dirhams. Similarly, Zakat has also to be paid on buried treasures, mines etc, one-fifth. However, stones are exempted and those mines situated within the precincts of one's home.

To whom charity to be given?

Sura IX states in detail the persons who are eligible to receive charity. "Alms shall be used only for the advancement of Allah's cause, for the ransom of captives and debtors, and for distribution among the poor, the destitute, the wayfarers, those that are employed in collecting alms, and those that are converted to the faith." The Tradition deals extensively with seven categories of persons who could only receive alms.

1. *Needy or Fakhir* i.e., those who possess property but not sufficient enough for their use and out of this they need not give alms(Nisab).
2. *Poor or Miskin* i.e., those who do not have any property.
3. *Slaves* as ransom to set them free.
4. *Debtors* for clearing their debts.
5. *Muqaddis* or Collectors of Alms.
6. *Fighters* or *Fi Saili 'Llah* i.e., those who are in the religious warfare, and
7. Travellers.

Exempted from receiving any alms are the members from the Prophet's family. It is told that one day Prophet had made his grand children, Imams Hassan and Hussain to omit a few dates eaten by them, as the fruits were given in charity. This injunction is even now scrupulously followed by the Hashmites—they accept no alms but however gifts are allowed to them.

FOURTH PILLAR OF ISLAM

Saum (Fasting)

The fourth practical duty obligatory to the Faithful is Fasting during Ramadan, the ninth month of the Islamic lunar calendar. Fast is saum in Arabic meaning the abandoning of the cravings of food for Allah's sake. Fasting is "the gate of religion" also described as a shield, an atonment for sin. It has three degrees. 1. Restraint of the stomach and of physical restraint i.e., the restraint of the stomach and other parts of the body from hunger and other wants, 2. Restraint of the senses i.e., the restriant of eyes, ears, tongue from seeing, hearing and telling of sins and vices, 3. Restraint of the heart from all wordly cares and solely think of Allah and seek His protection.

Mark the concluding remark which gives the purpose of fasting.

Why fasting is ordained on Muslims? It is prescribed to the community of Believers so that they "may learn self-restraint." Fasting is a Taqwa, a shield, a protector to guard oneself (from sins and offences) by restraining himself from doing sins by voluntarily foregoing some of the lawful things for fear of slipping into trouble with the unlawful. In other words, the faster keeps away from eating, drinking, smoking, sexual intercourse etc. which are otherwise lawful acts. This voluntary restraint has a multi effect on the fasters. Firstly, it increases his Will Power in controlling his wordly desires. He never becomes sensual. Secondly, fasting strenghens belief. When one is fasting, he voluntarly suffers thirst and hunger along with the poor and is more prone to think of his creator and His attributes. Thirdly, it levels him with the common man. Every Muslim whether a king or a Shaikh, a trader or the poorest of the poor learns to suffer hunger and thirst by fasting. It alone inculcates in them the habit of helping the poor. That is the reason almsgiving is elevated to an almost obligatory duty especially on twenty-seventh of Ramadan. Fasting and distribution of Zakat—these are the two glories of Ramadan.

Fasting during Ramadan is based on the express injunction contained in Sura II verses 180-187. "Believers for you fasting is decreed as it was decreed for those before you; perchance you will guard yourselves against evil. Fast a certain number of days, but if any one of you is ill or on a journey let him fast a similar number of days later on; and for those that can afford it there is a ransom;[1] the feeding of a poor man. He that does good of his own accord shall be well rewarded; but to fast is better for you, if you but knew it. In the month of Ramadan, the Quran was revealed a book of guidance with proofs of guidance distinguishing right from wrong. Therefore whoever of you is present in that month let him fast. But he who is ill or on a journey shall fast a similar number of days later on." Ramadan is one of the most important months of Islamic calender. Of its excellence, it is believed that a transcript of the Quran was descended to the lowest heaven in this month. From there, it was revealed to Muhammad. It is also in one of the days of this month known as Laylat al-Qadar[2] (exact day is not known. May be any of the odd days from 21st to

---

[1]The meaning is variously interperted. Some even say that people are at liberty to fast or not. However it was abrogated and all those who shall be present (at home) in this month, fast the same month. This perhaps excludes suckling women.

[2]Night of power. The Orthodox believe that on a certain moment of the night all the animals, vegetables and trees bow down before God and all the waters of the ocean become sweet for a brief period.

27th Ramadan) that the fate of human being is determined. "Here in descend the angels and the spirit by permission of their Lord in every matter, and in all peace till the breaking of the morn." (Sura XCVI). Tradition ascribes to Muhammad the saying,"when the month of Ramadan arrives, the gates of paradise are open, and the gates of hell are shut, and the devils are chained by the leg, and that only those who deserve it (Ramadan) will be permitted to enter at the gate of heaven called Raiyan."[1] With the approach of the first night of Ramadan, all the devils and the rebellious jinns are chained for the rest of the month. Of its other importance, Prophet Muhammad received the first revelation on the twenty-fourth night of this month when he was meditating alone in the cave of Hira, near Mecca. It is on this night Gabriel made his appearance with the Divine Message, "Read, in the name of Your Lord, who has created all things, who has created man from clots of blood."
"Read, Your Lord is the Most Bountiful One who taught the use of the pen; who taught man that which he did not know."

Such is the excellence of Ramadan and fasting is compulsory to all the Muslims except the sick, infirm, pregnant and suckling women, travellers who are on a journey of more than three days, and young children who are below the age of puberty. However, as expiation (Quza), the sick and the travellers can observe an equal number of fasts later when they are fit to observe it. In lieu of fasting, distributing expiatory alms (Fidya) is also permitted.

Ramadan is the Fourth Pillar on which the magnificent mansion of Islam is built on. It inculcates in the Faithfuls an urge to do right. It teaches them to be good not only in this month but throughout the year. Ramadan reminds them of their responsibilities towards fellow beings. Like Salat, like Pilgrimage like all other Islamic institutions, the rich too is ordained to know the rigours of life, the pangs of hunger and thirst. A remedy too is suggested—to share their wealth with the poor. During Ramadan, many devout Muslims invite the poor for meals. Ramadan shows their resolute faith in Allah and strengthens their faith.

The month is so called from Ramz meaning to burn. The popular belief is that fasting will burn away the sins of men (Ghiyasu'l Lughah) and hence the month on which it occurs is called Ramazan[2] On the

---

[1]There are 8 doors in Paradise and through one of which called Raiyan, the faster shall enter.

[2]In English it is written Ramadan.

basis of this belief, many Muslims, eventhough they are not strict about the prescribed daily liturgical prayers, fast during Ramadan. Another probability for the origin of the word is that in ancient times Ramadan always occurred during the hot season.[1] There is a prophetic saying, "That a fast of one day in a sacred month is better than a fast of thirty days in another month, and that the fast of one day in Ramadan is more meritorius than a fast of thirty days in a sacred month." Eventhough fasting in general is good, it is unlawful on five days—the Feast of the Breaking of the Fast (Id al Fitr), the Kine-Fete, (Great Festival) and the 11th, 12th and 13th of the twelfth month of the year.

Ramadan has several other names. The Scholars count nearly sixty names, among others the Month of Allah, the Month of al-Quran, the Month of Salvation, the Month of Good, the Month of Welfare etc.

Because Islamic Calendar is Lunar, the months occur in rotation in all seasons. When Ramadan falls in the hot season, the day long fast is extremely tiresome for not a drop of water is drunk during the day; also 20 additional Ra'ka or Forms of Prayer (Tarawih) must be gone through after the night prayer. It is customary for pious Muslims to stay for considerable time in the mosques especially for the last ten days reading the Quran and refraining from conversation on wordly matters.

Fasting is to be kept during daytime i.e., the fasters must abstain from eating, drinking and smoking during the period from dawn to sunset. Fasting becomes void if the faster smells perfumes or applies sweet smelling ointment or if he kisses or touches a woman with passion and desire. However, it is lawful if one approaches his wife on the night. "It is now lawful for you on the night of the fast to lie with your wives, they are a garment unto you, and ye are a garment unto them." (Sura II.Cow) Similarly, if any food larger than a grain of corn enters the body or remain in the mouth from the night meal and swallowed also break the fast. The Traditional interpretation of sunrise is that time of the morning when a white thread can be distinguished from a black thread in the pre-dawn sky. But in the real sense fasting begins with a Niyya or Intention of the Saum and continues until the sun sets in the western horizon. Niyya is usually said after a collation meal before the Dawn (Suhur) is eaten. The recommended things to break the fast (Iftar) are water, Sherbet or with a little salt or Date fruits or any other light drinks before the performance of Maghrib Prayer. In imitating the

---

[1]The Sword of Islam. A. N. Wollastan. p. 317.

practice of the Prophet, many religious Muslims prefer to eat a Date or a bit of salt to break fast. It is preferred to eat an odd number of dates—1,2,3, etc. The prayer is followed by a light meal (Fatur). Observing a twenty-ra'ka worship known as Salat Al-Tarawih led by Imam after Isha prayer is specially recommended. There is a prophetic saying," The person who says the nightprayers of the Ramadan shall be pardoned all his past sins and the person who says the prayers on the Lailatul Qudar with faith and the hope of reward shall be pardoned of all his past sins." The fast on twenty-seventh Ramadan is equally meritorious and many good Muslims calculate the Zakat to be paid by them on the basis of their yearly income and distribute it to the poor.

Mere fasting has no meaning, unless the faster does not abstain from all gossips and idle talks. In fact, fasting demands from the fasters good conduct. They should cultivate their minds to good thoughts, pious talks and noble deeds. Fasting without a simultaneous spiritual awakening is no more than abstaining from hunger and thirst. God does not accept such careless fasting from impious fasters. Prophet said, "when you fast, let your tongue and every eye and ear and hand, in short every limb of your body, also fast. A great many who fast get nothing from their fasting save hunger and thirst, and many wake up nights and get nothing from it save the waking up."

Saum is continued for one full month till the sighting of the moon of shawal. Next day is celebrated all over the Muslimdom as one of the two important festivals. It is known as Id al-Fitr (The Festival of the Breaking of the Fast).[1] Id means,"Returning Day", that is the day repeats every year to commemorate the Fast of Ramadan. It is enjoined upon the Faithfuls who are above poverty line to give Charity (Sadaqah) to the poor. This is compulsory to all the Muslims, fasters and non-fasters and all those who are dependent on them. This charity is called Id Charity or Fitrah must be distributed to individual Muslims (and not to any organisation, institutions or government) on the morning of the Festival before the Id prayer. Further, fasting of a non-paying, member of charity will not be acceptable to God. It is thus that the charity is distributed, the Faithfuls gather in an open ground (Idgah) for the 2-ra'ka congregational worship. When the prayer is over, the Imam addresses the gathering with a Khutbah oration stressing the importance of the day. This is followed by a Munajat for God's Blessings

---

[1]Other names are Id al-Ramadan, Sadaqah or Feast of Alms, Idu's Saghir or the Minor Festival.

for the pardon of the sins, for good rain, harvest etc. It ends with the Imam making a supplication for the people. Before the congregation departs for home, they greet each other. The rest of the day is celebrated with feasts and a lot of merry making. Children wear their best, specially bought for the occasion, anoint their bodies with perfumes and visit their relations.

Based on the Sunnah, the community of Believers perform the **Id-al-Fitr on any open ground, need not necessarily be on a mosque** to display their strength and superiority of Islam's cult. This was essential especially for the nascent Islamic Community when the few converts were attacked by the rebels. As it was then, it is even now followed scrupulously. It is highly praised for those who could not participate in the Festival Worship, especially the children and women to watch the congregation praying. It is for this reason to show Islam's strength that Prophat Muhammad used to take different routes, going on one route and returning by another for Id Prayers. The Prophet on such festival occasions used to go round the congregation asking them 'Give alms, give alms' He never failed to meet the women assemblage for the same purpose. He too used to wear special clothes with red or green strips.

Besides obligatory Fasting mentioned above, every Muslim is expected to observe voluntary fasts (Saum't Tatawwu) on the following days.

1. One day fast on the tenth day of Muhurram i,e., the Day of Ashura. Other recommended fasts during Muhurram are Thursdays, Fridays and Saturdays and the first day of Muhurram. The Prophet is reported to have said,"Those who fast on Thursday, Friday and Saturday of this month shall be removed from hell fire a distance of 700 years journey and those who fast on the first day of the month shall be kept from sin for the next two years." Such is the excellence of Muhurram.

2. Six days fast following Id al-Fitr.

3. Weekly two days fast on every Monday and Thursday.

4. If possible in the whole of Shaban or some part of the month.

Fifteenth Shaban is one of the sacred days of Islam. Known as Shabi-Barat or Night of Record, the devout Muslims keep an all-night vigil on the strength of belief that God registers all the actions of mankind for the following year on this day. Fasting on the day and offering special hundred rak's prayer in the night has special reward.

5. Fast on Bright Days (Al-Ayyam Biz) i.e., 13th, 14th and 15th of

every month.

6. Fasting on alternate days. Prophet David was believed to have fasted on alternate days and kept a very good health.

7. Fasting in Rajab, the most honoured month is also recommended to the pious Muslims.

FIFTH PILLAR OF ISLAM

Haj or Pilgrimage

Pilgrimage or Haj (Hadj) is the fifth and last ritual duty prescribed to the Community of Believers. Haj is essentially an international gathering, the only one of its kind any religion has made to its votaries compulsory. Serving as a pan-Islamic forum where Muslims of all races assemble in the very cradle of Islam to perform jointly certain rites in and around the House of Allah, it is the most important ceremony of Islam. This assembly of a hundred thousand devotees in Islam's first city is great indeed. Trade is brisk during the season. Catering assumes a new magnitude. Not in use the ancient caravan route across the desert which was once the life-line of Arabia, the pilgrimage is the only occasion when the Meccans could continue their trading activity. They thus lend rooms, guide the pilgrims and serve food to them, hire mounts, sell sacred water and wares brought from all parts of the world. At least for some time of the year, it functions as an international market where buyers from all over the world come to select goods from all countries.

Haj proper is the observance of certain rites in and around Ka'ba and in other religiously important places of Arafat, Muzdalifa and Mina during the first ten days of Dul Haj, the twelfth month of Islamic calendar. Any visit to these places on any other day for performance of these sacred rites is Umra or Lesser Pilgrimage.[1] However, the Umra performed immediately before the commencement of Haj is called Qiran and that of any other day, Tamattu.

Divine injunction on Pilgrimage can be read in several Quranic passages, especially the verses 27-28 of Sura XXII (The Pilgrimage) and verses 196 of Sura II (Cow) are important.[2]

---

[1] Till 1184, Umra was observed as a separate ceremony. But now it is being supererogatory rite to be performed at any time except the first ten days of Dul-Haj.

[2] For other Quranic passages, read Sura III, Sura V. etc.

"Exhort all men to make the pilgrimage. They will come to you on foot and on backs of swift camels from every distant quarter; they will come to avail themselves of many a benefit to pronounce on the appointed days the name of Allah over the beasts which He has given them. Eat of their flesh yourselves, and feed the poor and the unfortunate."

"Then let the pilgrims spruce themselves, make their vows, and circle the Ancient House. Such is Allah's commandment. He that reverses the sacred rites of Allah shall fare better in the sight of his Lord."(Sura XXII).

"Make the pilgrimage and visit the Sacred House for His sake. If you cannot, send such offerings as you can afford and do not shave your heads until the offerings have reached their destination. But if any of you is ill or suffers from an ailment of the dead, he must pay a ransom either by fasting or by alms-giving or by offering a sacrifice.

If in peacetime any one of you combines the visit with the pilgrimage, he must offer such gifts as he can afford, but if he lacks the means let him fast three days during the pilgrimage and seven when he has returned; that is, ten days in all. That is incumbent on him whose family are not present at the Holy Mosque. Have fear of Allah, know that He is stern in retribution. Make the pilgrimage in the appointed months. He that intends to perform it in those months must abstain from Sexual intercourse, obscene language, and acrimonious disputes while on pilgrimage. Allah is aware of whatever good you do. Provide yourselves well the best provision is piety. Fear Me, then, you that are endowed with understanding." (Sura II)

"Pilgrimage is a duty towards God for all who can make the journey" (Sura II Imrans). It is variously interpreted. The most received opinion is that pilgrimage is compulsory for all those who have the provision for the journey and a beast to ride upon. According to Al Shafi it means all those who have enough money if they cannot go themselves, must hire some other to perform it on their behalf. Malik ibn Abu includes all those who are healthy and can bear the fatigue of the journey on foot, if he has no beast to ride, who can earn their living on the way. Abu Hanifa says all those who have money and healthy to undergo the ordeal.

Haj is compulsory for all healthy adults who have means to meet the expenses of the journey after making provision for their families during their absence from home. Its omission by such well to do persons is equal to Kabirah or Great Sin and so it is enjoined upon all rich and healthy Muslims to perform it at least once in their lifetime. Sick persons and those without means are exempted from the ordeal. Participation of women is conditional i.e. if unaccompanied by any responsible male member is discouraged. But they could perform the Haj accompanied by their husbands or guardians or near relatives (Muharam) who are within the prohibited degrees of marriage.

To understand the various rites connected with the Annual pilgrimage, we should have some knowledge of the historical importance of the sacred places associated with Haj. The first and foremost of these places is Mecca, the very palladium of Islam. It is here, where the soil is sanctified by the preachings of many earlier Prophets that Muhammad was born. Its shrine known as Bait Allah, that is the House of Allah was the nucleus of the religious life of the entire inhabitants of Arabia. The Arabs for and near venerated it as the original Prayer House built by Abraham and his son Ismael. Another Arab Tradition traces its origin to Adam who feeling the necessity to have a sacred house for the purpose of worship built Ka'ba in imitation of Baitul Mamur, the Sacred Prayer House in Paradise. The original house was destroyed in the Great Deluge. Another popular legend is that the house built by Adam was taken to Paradise but his son, Seth raised in its site another house. It was this Ka'ba which was lost in the Flood. For many centuries the site was untraceable until Abraham came to Mecca discovered it and rebuilt the House. Simple in structure, the Ka'ba as built by Abraham had no roof and to mark the starting point, he placed the Black Stone which was supposed to have been brought to him by Gabriel. The next house was constructed by the Amalekites or the descendants of Shem, the son of Noah. When it showed signs of ruins, Jorhamites built a new house which was renovated by the Qusai in the fifth century. The sacred edifice for the first time had a roof of palm leaves. When this was seriously damaged in a flood during the time of Prophet, under the supervision of the Quraish it was renovated, heightened the walls and made some more alterations and additions with the material obtained from a shipwreck.

It was during this time that an event happened which made the Prophet an arbiter in a dispute among the Meccans for the coveted honour of placing the Black Stone in its wall. Dispute was heard by the Prophet, Al-Amin and his verdict earned him laurels from all the disputants. All of them jointly raised the Sacred Stone in its proper place, helped by the Prophet. The Sacred House came as quickly and the erstwhile edifice soon became serviceable, but alas, in an unprecedented fire in the year 683 A.D the Black Stone broke into three pieces.[1] Thereupon Abdulla ibn Zubair widened it by 7 cubits[2] more in length and 9 cubits in height which was, within ten years on public protest rebuilt by Hajjaj ibn Yusuf. In another violent storm in 1620, the Ka'ba was almost swept away and many of its lamp posts were razed to the ground, much of its walls were destroyed in the flood. However, it was given an extensive repair and renovation lasting for ten years. The present Ka'ba dates back from this period. Thus rebuilt and renovated from time to time the present structure is cub-shaped measuring 12x10 metres and 12 metres made of undressed stone. The whole structure is built over a marble of 25 centimetre thickness. To drain the rain water from the roof, it has a water spout made of solid gold obviously the only ornamentation in the entire building. Covering the walls of the Ka'ba is a black vesture (Kiswa) specially made by the ruler of Egypt and brought in great procession accompanied by a ceremonial palanquine of the ruler (Mahal). This custom is dispensed with.

Quranic verses are embroidered in the Kiswa on a height coinciding the girdle of the Ka'ba. Prior to the commencement of Haj, between 25 and 28 of Dul Kad, the black Kiswa is removed and a white one, matching the colour of the Ihram dress of the Pilgrim is put on. This will be removed at the conclusion of Haj and Ka'ba will have a new black Kiswa.

The most important of its four corners is the south-east corner wherein is set high enough for the pious to touch and kiss the Black Stone (Hajrul Aswad). The circuit around the Ka'ba (Tawaf) always begins in this corner with a ceremonial kissing of the stone if possible. The only door of the Ka'ba is situated to the right of Hajrul Aswad about 2 metres above the ground connected by a movable three-step ladder. A depression in the pavement in front of the door is believed by the Believers as the though in which Abraham mixed mortar when he was building the Sacred House. Yamani corner is next in importance. There is another stone held to be sacred not as sacred as the Black Stone in the Yamani Corner. The Pilgrims touch it as they go round al-Ka'ba. The other two are the Iraqi Corner and the Syrian Corner. At a little distance from al-Ka'ba is a pavilion enclosing a stone

---

[1] It is held together by silver frame. The stone measures 40 centimetre in diametre.

[2] 1 cubit = 55.8 c.m.

slab revered as the structure on which Abraham stood supervising the construction of the sacred building. The devotees even now see the foot prints of Abraham on its surface. Known as Maqam Ibrahim, the Pilgrims give considerable importance to it. They pray a two-rakat prayer behind the Pavilion of Abraham as an important part of Haj rites. Outside the Maqam is the marble pulpit used by the Imam to deliver the Friday Sermon. Leaving an open passage in between the Iraqi and Syrian corner is a semi circular wall (Hijr) containing the graves of Hajar and Ismael. The house around the Sacred well, Zamzan believed to have been miraculously found in the depth of the desert and slaked the thirst of Ismael and Hajar is situated exactly opposite the Yamani Corner. The paved courtyard intersperse with path ways, and centering the Ka'ba and the Sacred wall extends to an area measuring 100 x160 metres. In the outer extermity of the courtyard has several arches with twenty-two doors, the two important being Bab-al Salam and Bab al-Safa in the north-east and south respectively. Bab al-Safa is the exit, opening to the Sacred hillock of al-Safa. It is through this door that the pilgrims reach for the rites of running the distance between al-Safa and al-Marwa.

The limits of the Sacred territory of Mecca are marked with Minar like pillars about six miles from Mecca. The Arab Tradition narrates a story how satan stopped himself by seeing the fire lit by Abraham on the hilltop of Abu Qubays dominating Mecca. The present pillars marking the sacred land of Mecca are built over the spots where satan was surprised by the fire and declined to go further. At present there are five similar stages marked. The pilgrims approaching Mecca stop at these pillars to change to the Holy garb (Ihram) as a mark of sanctification.

Arafa is a plain with hills on one side about four hours camel ride distance from Mecca. The Traditional belief is that Adam and Eve met each other in Arafa after the descent from Paradise. In the top of the hill is the Jabal Al-Rahma (Mt. of Mercy). Standing there the Prophet had addressed a sermon to his people. In imitation of this, the devotees assemble in the hill to hear a sermon in the afternoon of the ninth day of Dul-Haj called Wuquf. This is one of the essential rites of Haj. Mina is a valley almost half-way from Mecca to Arafa. While returning from Arafa and on reaching Mina on the tenth of Dul-Haj, the pilgrims perform the essential closing rites of the Pilgrimage. Muzdalifa is another valley situated between Arafa and Mina where the pilgrims pass the tenth night of Dul-Haj.

With this outline of the description of the Sacred places of Mecca, we shall now return to the consideration of the essential rites of Haj.

As we shall see pillars are built marking the holy ground of Mecca. On reaching any one of them, the devotees after taking a bath, recite a 2-ra'ka prayer, discard the garments to a white seamless one namely Ihram similar to the costume supposed to have been worn by Abraham. It consists of Izar measuring six feet by three and a half feet broad Lower garment around the loin reaching above the knees tuck at the middle and the Rida also measuring 6ft x 3ft. Upper garment covering the shoulder keeping the right hand bare, knotted at the right side. In the feet, they wear simple leather footwears called Nal. (Wearing shoes, boots are not recommended). Carrying an umbrella to avoid heat is allowed. Ihram is not compulsory for women. By wearing Ihram, they get into a state of sanctity till the last essential rite is performed. The pilgrims in Ihram are called Muhrim. So, certain acts are taboo to the pilgrims. They are sexual intercourse, perfuming the body, paring the nails etc. Hunting and killing are also prohibited during the pilgrimage. However, one can get rid of biting creatures like kites, crows, rats, scorpions, dogs etc. Thus sanctified themselves, the pilgrims say the Intention (Niya) of the Pilgrimage. It is also possible to make the Niya, any time preceding two months of Dul Haj. Facing Mecca, they say aloud, "I vow this Ihram of Haj and the Umra to Allah Almighty.' They then recite the Talbiya or Formula, as follows.

> *"Labbayka! Ya Rabbi Labbayka*
> *Labbayka! La Sharika Laka labbayka!*
> *Inanl-Hamda Wa' ni'mata laka!*
> *Wa' l mulka La Sharika laka!"*
> *(Here I am, O God! Here I am. No Partner hast Thou, Here I am.*
> *Verily praise and beneficence are thine, and the kingdom No partner hast Thou, Here am I.)*

Reciting the formula as often as possible, the pilgrims enter the Holy city and then through marked out routes, they assemble in the mosque. When the Ka'ba is sighted, they utter. "O, Allah! increase all those who have honoured it and glorified it, the Hajis[1] and Mutamirs[2] with degree and greatness and honour and dignity." Then the new comers

---

[1] Hajis One who successfully performed Haj.

[2] Mutamir. One who successfully performed Umra.

sacred building. With right foot first, they enter the mosque through the Bab al-Salam. On reaching the sacred precincts of al-Ka'ba they go to the south-east corner to kiss the sacred Black-stone. If they could not go near the stone because of crowd, they touch it with their fingers or walking sticks and kiss that part. Having thus kissed the sacred stone, they move to the right and go round the Ka'ba touching the Yamani corner (Sura CXXII.27). On completion of the first circuit, they touch the Black Stone and kiss it before the second circuit is done. Thus they complete seven circuits, the first three being in quick steps and the others walking or with slow steps. Having thus completed the Tawaf, they go behind Maqam Ibrahim to recite the verse 119 (Sura II) and then to pray two rak'a. This is followed by touching the Black Stone and kissing it. Then they leave the mosque through Bab al-Safa to perform the rite called Sa'y[1]. They formulate the Niya of Sa'y and climb the mount al-Safa. While ascending they recite the Takbir and on reaching the top of the hill, they turn towards Ka'ba and pray to pardon the past sins. "O my Lord, pardon and pity and pass over that sin which Thou knowest. Verily Thou knowest what is not known, and verily Thou art the Most Glorious, the Most Generous, O our Lord! grant us in this world prosperity, and in the future prosperity, and save us from the punishment of fire." Having said the prayer of Pardon thrice, the devotees descend and with swinging strides they reach the foot of Mt.. Marwa and climb the hill. Then back and forth, the pilgrims run seven times repeating all the while the formula, "Labbayka Ya Rabbi Labbayka!" Encompassing the Safa and Marwa is sanctioned by divine revelation. "Safa and Marwa are monuments of God. It shall be no offence for the pilgrim or visitor to the Sacred House to walk around them" (Sura II. The Cow)

Having thus completed the Sa'y at al-Marwa with the seventh circuit, the pilgrims who perform Umra shave their heads as a mark of the termination of the pilgrimage, change the Ihram. Those who perform Haj proper have to observe many more rites. The essential rites of the Haj begin from the seventh day of Dul-Haj. In a sermon before the Salat al-Zuhr on the seventh day of Dul-Haj, the devotees hear a

---

[1]Sa'y is performed commemorating the run of Hajar in search of water in between the two hills. Another popular belief is that the Meccans ridiculed the disciples of the Prophet saying that the climate of Medina had ruined the Meccan refugees and they had lost the health. To disprove it, they ran the distance and proved that they were as healthy as any one in Mecca.

gist of the Haj rites and its importance. On the next day, that is eighth of Dul-Haj known as Yaum al-Tarawiya (so called because the devotees must lay in a supply of water for himself) they set out for Arafa passing through Mina. Stopping there for the mid-day prayer, the Believers remain there till the dawn of the next day. Continuing the journey, they reach Arafa before the afternoon of the ninth day for it is in the afternoon that Wuquf of Arafa, the most important rite of Haj takes place. There he stands erect in submission to the Will of Allah reciting the pious formula, often reciting,"Labbayka Ya Rabbi Labbayka!" With the approach of the time that is after the crossing of the sun in the meridian, the Imam ascends the Sacred Hill of Arafa in a camel to deliver the most important sermon of Haj, standing exactly in the same place where the Prophet stood to deliver a Sermon to his followers in the year 632 A.D. The pilgrims stand attentively listening to the Kutba. This is called Khutbatu'l Waqfah (The Sermon of Standing). After the Asr and Maghrib worships are said there, the pilgrims move out of Arafa for Muzdalifa, a valley mid-way between Mina and Arafa. This is probably the only dangerous part of the entire pilgrimage, for hundred thousand pilgrims move out of the hill taking the same route, to the sacred valley of Mina, often accompanied by gunshots and display of fire works. This swift movement is called Iftida. Night is spent in Muzdalifa. Each of the pilgrim picks up several pebbles for use in a later stage of the pilgrimage. Before dawn of the tenth day, the pilgrims proceed to Mina to perform the last rite. There in the slope of the valley, they stop to cast one pebble each they had collected from Muzdalifa and carefully kept with them all through the journey, to Jamrat al-Aqiba[1] symbolising the great satan. Throwing is accompanied by the utterance, "Bismillahi, Allahu Akbar!" (In the name of Allah, Allah is great.") and blown upon it. Seven pebbles are thrown at the largest pillar, a dwarf buttress of masonry about 8 feet high and 2 feet broad symbolising the Great Satan. This is a rite, so goes a legend perpetuating the memory of Abraham driving away the Satan at this place, when the grand old patriarch was dissuaded from sacrificing his son to God.

Having thus cast the seven pebbles, they return to sacrifice a beast which must be any fully grown blemishless goat, sheep, cow or camel. Keeping the head of the animal facing the Ka'ba, if possible the pil-

[1] Jamrah means Gravel. There are 3 such pillars, Al-Ula, Al-Wusta and Al-Aqibah, (the first, the middle and the Last respectively). The last one is also called Shaitanul Kabir or the Great Devil.

grims themselves cut its throat reciting the fomula "In the name of Allah, Allah is great." Taking a chunk of the flesh for themselves, the remainder is given to the poor in charity. Quite appropriately, the tenth day of Dul-Haj is known as Yaum al-Nahr or Day of Sacrifice. It is followed by a feast. Because of this, the day is also called Id al-Adha. With it, the essential rites of the pilgrimage came to an end. To mark the successful culmination of Haj, the pilgrims shave the head, pare the nails. Those who are sick or suffering from any ailment of the head, can pay a ransom either by fasting three days, or feeding six poor people or sacrificing a sheep. From then on, they are in a state of Tahallul Al-Saghir for they are free of minor prohibitions. The only prohibited things now are perfumes and sexual connections. They hasten to al-Kaba for performing the final circuits (Tawaf al-Ifada). With it, all the major rites are over and the pilgrims are fully and finally desanctified. That is, they are in a state of Tahallul Al-Kabir. But before departing for home, they return to Mina to spend the 11th, 12th, and 13th of Dul Haj there. This is called Ayyam Al-Tashriq, the period of waiting for the sacrificial meat to get dried in the sun. Jamrat al-Awusta is daily visited to cast seven stones[1] at it. Very few pilgrims return home from Mina before visiting Mecca for the "Farewell Circuits" and to drink from Zamzam. The sacred water is bottled and carried home. At home, it is shared by many. Some even keep it as a rare possession. It is drunk as a health tonic.

As we have seen, there are three most essential points for the lawful completion of Haj viz. wearing of pilgrim's garb or Ihram, to make the circuit round the Ka'ba, and standing in Arafat to listen to the Sermon (Qutba). Adding to this is the necessity to keep aloof from sexual intercourse during the period of Haj. Omission of any one of them, annuls Haj. There are five more acts whose observance is equally important for the successful completion of Haj. Its omission however does not invalidate the Haj as a whole. Their performance is rewarded. These five acts are.

1. Running between the two hills of Safa and Marwa,
2. Standing in Muzdalifa,
3. Casting pebbles at Mina,
4. To make an additional circuit around Ka'ba (Tawaf), and
5. To shave the head as a mark of culmination of Haj.

[1] Shaffis throw in all 49 pebbles—7 on the tenth day, 21 each on the 11th and 12th day. Hanafis besides this 49, throw 21 stones on the 13th day making a total of 70. However 7 of these stones must be collected from Muzdalifa and the rest from Mina. The stones must be washed 7 times.

The other failures or non-observance are minor and expiation (Kaffara) by additional sacrifices or giving alms to the poor or by fasting makes up the deficiency.

Not only for the participants of the Haj, for the entire Muslim world, the conclusion of the Pilgrimage is a great day. Known as the Feast of Sacrifice, it is the greatest Festival of Muslims, who on this day offer special prayers followed by a sermon on the importance of the Day and the merit earned by Sacrifice. Usually, the pious kill a sheep, cow, goat or camel depending on his capacity, and distribute the meat to the poor, keeping one-third for himself and family, and another third to the relations. The sacrifice is made with great solemnity. Turning the head of the animal towards Al-Ka'ba chanting,"In the name of the great God! verily my prayers, my sacrifice, my life, my death, He has no partner: that is what I am bidden, for I am first those who are Muslims," the animal is slaughtered, cutting the vein on the neck with a sharp knife.

It is recommended to visit the Mosque of the Prophet at Medina after the completion of Haj. The devotees enter Medina after legal purification. When the dome of the Mosque is sighted, they say some pious ejaculation and then enter the mosque with the right foot foremost. In the mosque they perform 4-ra'ka prayer. There is special reward for those who recite Sura 109 (The Unbeliever) and Sura 112. Having prayed thus, they move to the western window of the Hujra to say an Invocation to the Apostle who is interred there. Then they go back to the mosque to pray another 4-ra'ka prayer. When this is over, they go to the window facing the tomb of Abu Bakr to address an Invocation to the first Successor of the Prophet. Similarly, they pray on the tombs of Umar, and Fatima who is interned in a room adjoining the Hujra. This completes all the rites in Medina but one, the Departure Salutation. The devotees now enter the Porch, and say the Departure Salutation before departing.

At home, a heroe's welcome awaits the successful participants of the Annual Pilgrimage (Haj). The sacred water which they bring from the Holy Zamzām passes through all the mouths, the Dates are eaten by many. The episode of the long journey, its perils and advantages, its ups and downs, the story of the Pilgrimage is shared by all.